Buchanan Remembered

Edited by Jennifer Taggart

Published by Buchanan Community Council
with financial assistance from the Heritage Lottery Fund

Published in 2007 by Buchanan Community Council
Passfoot Cottage, Balmaha, Stirlingshire G63 OJQ
www.buchanan-lochlomond.com

British Library Cataloguing-in-Publication Data:
A catalogue record of this book is available from the British Library.

ISBN 978-0-9555691-0-4

Printed in Scotland by Thos McGilvray & Son Ltd, Wemyss Road, Dysart, Fife, KY1
2XZ

Cover Illustrations
Front Cover: Balmaha Bay. Painted by Kirsty Twaddle
Back cover: Walter McAllister, champion, Buchanan Sheepdog Trials.
Photo by Willie Simpson

Foreword
James Graham, Eighth Duke of Montrose

Looking at a book of the Rentals in Buchanan in 1724 it is striking the number of surnames that are still present in the district, both common ones and those that are fairly unusual. There is a strong sense that we have all managed to rub along together through all the many patterns of history.

The first historical record of the name Graham in the area is 1325 when Sir David Graham, the owner at that time, completed an exchange of Inchcailleach and Inchfad with Robert the Bruce for other titles, much of the land on the east side of the Loch being Graham lands until purchased by Patrick the 14th Laird of Buchanan in 1460.

This has been one of the parts of Scotland that have contained in one community both the highlands and the lowlands with all their contrasts. But it also benefited in the days before proper roads from its watery connection to the Clyde Valley and all its developments. Who can tell at this time whether those who endeavoured to extract pig iron in the bloomeries along the eastern shore were highlanders or lowlanders?

We are now entering a period with a great sense of general cooperation and mutual involvement which will be a good test of our present day sense of community. We might consider as a note of caution that in a previous era an attempt along these lines to build a statutory road from Drymen to Rowardennan had to be abandoned for a lack of willingness of all concerned to participate in the hard work involved in such a community project.

The idea of a central landed estate, which was required to provide most of the needs and services of the community, has long been abandoned. We now look to the Scottish Executive and its institutions to provide for most of what we need. But there is still an essential level where the community is the only framework in which individuals, their care and concerns can really be satisfied.

i

Preface

Seonaidh Bannerman
Chairman, Buchanan Community Council

Since the Millennium, Buchanan Community Council has been discussing ways of marking this milestone of the turning centuries. About three years ago the idea of a history was mentioned, a living history that would capture the memories of some members of the community who have lived and worked here all their lives, perhaps with a few who have either come here to make a life, or who have gone away after a childhood in Buchanan.

We were fortunate in persuading Dr Jennifer Taggart to undertake this living history on behalf of our community. The project involves many elderly persons, some of whom are now housebound. For some, it is the first serious writing they have ever attempted. Jenny has searched out contributions over a wide age range, from eight to ninety-eight.

Our community is scattered over a wide geographic area, and there is a growing number of holiday homes. Projects such as this help a community to maintain a positive and developing idea of itself. I hope it will be the first of many.

I hope you enjoy reading the book and pass it on to others, especially those who have left our community to make their lives furth of Scotland. This book will preserve and enhance their memories.

Editor's Introduction

Jenny Taggart

I was delighted when the Community Council asked me to put together a book about people in Buchanan Parish. Chrissie Bannerman and I had often talked about the need for such a book, and I trust she will not be disappointed by what follows.

The official history of Buchanan is well recorded. Its scenery is instantly recognisable the world over. But little has been written about the daily lives of the local people. When I came to live in the area I was immediately struck by the strong and active sense of community in Buchanan, and this living history gives powerful supporting evidence.

All contributors volunteered their services. They were asked to write, in their own words, about their families, their work and the events that had shaped their lives. The result is this remarkably varied collection of memories, tales and anecdotes. A condition of the Lottery grant was that the book had to be published within a calendar year. Despite this tight schedule, everyone whose contribution is included set to work with enthusiasm completing his or her task happily, and on time. Family photographs were searched out to help illustrate the book.

The contributions have been divided broadly into two types. The first five have been given individual titles. They set the scene within which the remaining more personal accounts are placed. These latter chapters are entirely individual in style and personal in content; they have been inserted alphabetically.

As the idea of the book took hold it became clear that there is much more to be told about Buchanan. Perhaps *Buchanan Remembered* will be the first of many?

Jennifer M Taggart

Acknowledgements

A book such as this could not be undertaken without the help of willing volunteers. Many people were involved in the production of *Buchanan Remembered*; it was truly a team effort. On behalf of Buchanan Community Council I would like to express my sincere thanks to all who played a part in this project.

Firstly, and most importantly, thanks are due to our forty contributors, without whom, there simply would have been no book. Your stories are wonderful.

James Taggart provided his computer skills and expertise. He spent countless hour organising text and photographs into book format, a complex and demanding task. I also want to record here a special thanks to James, my husband and friend, for the encouragement and support he has given me throughout.

Willie Simpson, photographer extraordinaire, donated over 120 outstanding photographs for the book and CD. His input helped make *Buchanan Remembered* come alive. Thanks a million, Willie.

The 'history group'- Chrissie Bannerman, Jenny Cronin, Peter Johnson, Angy MacFadyen, John Macfarlane, Glennys Nichols and Joe Twaddle - and numerous others - gave of their time and energy to approach and encourage contributors, many of who were shy about taking part. It was a great team effort.

Thanks are also due to Seonaidh Bannerman, Chairman of the Buchanan Community Council for initiating the project; Colin O'Brien, Provost of Stirling for his help in identifying funding sources; Seamus Graham, Duke of Montrose for agreeing to write the forward; Kirsty Twaddle for providing her beautiful painting of Balmaha Bay for our front cover; Iain Sommerville of Burntisland Heritage Trust who gave us advice and help on production; George Milne and Teresa Henderson at Thomas McGilvray & Son, Printers, who also gave valuable advice on production; and Awardsforall, part of the Heritage Lottery Fund, from which we received a grant of £5000 to cover our costs.

Jenny Taggart
Editor

Buchanan Remembered

Life on a Scottish Hill Farm
Chrissie Bannerman

Chrissie has been fortunate to have spent most of her adult life in one of the most beautiful places on earth and even more fortunate in the people she has lived amongst and worked with. Her children and grandchildren, Kate and Peter with their two children are in Glasgow, Seonaidh and Michelle and the twins and John are just up the road and Gilbert and Sheila in the cottage at Arrochybeg.

Photo: Chrissie Bannerman

Although not the most fertile of farms, the situation and the landscape of *The Old Manse* surely compensates. The hill ground runs from the Red Braes, over The Conich, onto MacKinlay Ridge and as far as The Gualann. There is some arable land between the foothills and Loch Lomond and wherever you stand on *The Old Manse* the Loch stretches out before you - one of the jewels in Scotland's crown.

John M Bannerman, the renowned Scottish rugby internationalist - and later Lord Bannerman of Kildonan - was factor to the Duke of Montrose and when he married Ray Mundell, a farmer's daughter from Sutherland in 1931, they took over the tenancy of *The Old Manse*. Here my husband, John, and his brother, Calum, and two sisters, Janet and Elizabeth, were brought up.

In 1968, sadly on the death of his father, John and I and our three children Kate, Mary and Seonaidh came back from Edinburgh to take over the farm. Gilbert was born after we returned and for a time John's mother and my father lived with us.

John continued to teach at Edinburgh University, coming home at weekends and until his retirement, the kindly and popular Jimmy Shanks, who had been shepherd here with John's father, managed the farm. Our children went to Buchanan Primary School and then to Balfron High School.

John M Bannerman with his sons John (L) and Calum (R).   *Photo: Chrissie Bannerman*

The farm carried the traditional hill stock - a flock of Scottish Blackface sheep and a herd of cross-hill cows, all of course out wintered. To me the farm year begins when the tups go out onto the hill in November and the hope is that the weather, during the weeks of the tupping season, is dry and crisp to keep the tups working. There is nothing more depressing than a long wet tupping season when the tups begin to straggle homewards, droukit and miserable and their work only half done. During our early years at *The Old Manse* the farms on the Lochside supported many more people and during the short winter days farmers and shepherds, with their collies, walked the hills keeping a watchful eye on the ewes. The cattle too, were fed daily and early in the year the calving started.

There was a lively social life in the village during those dark winter months with frequent dances and ceilidhs and whist drives. There was a flourishing Drama Club whose performances filled Buchanan Hall and later a Youth Club, the members of which, invited local people to their concerts and Burns Suppers to thank them for their support and those invitations were much coveted.

The Old Manse.   *Photo: Chrissie Bannerman*

Not only were there more people on the farms then but many also worked for the Forestry Commission and the Forestry houses were occupied by young families. One of the highlights of the season was what was known locally as The Sheepdog Dance – a name which occasioned raised eyebrows among those not in the know. There was an unspoken question. Do Sheepdogs really dance? It was the Annual Dinner Dance of The Buchanan Sheepdog Society held in the Rob Roy Motel in Aberfoyle and attended by the whole rural community. The menu was always the same. We started with Ravioli, followed by Chicken Chasseur then Black Forest Gateaux and it was just becoming fashionable to have wine with a meal - either a bottle of Blue Nun or a bottle of Mateus Rosé. This was followed by a very excellent dance with a good ceilidh band, and in those days everyone really knew how to dance. And inevitably there was a huge raffle. A very happy occasion.

However for the hill farms, all the social activities came to an end when the lambing started in mid-April but before lambing the ewes were gathered in off the hill for the Spring dip. This was very much a communal exercise. In those early days the other three Lochside farms, *Ben Lomond*, *Blairvockie* and *Cashel* were owned by the Department of Agriculture and the Forestry Commission and we neighboured with them and with the Duke's farms at *Moorpark* and *Gartincaber* as well as with two other Department farms in the Trossachs, *Corrie Grennan* and *Braeval*. This meant that all the farmers and shepherds, the two Donalds, Donald MacLean and Donald MacDermott from *Ben Lomond* and *Blairvockie*, Martin Pringle and Willie Simpson from *Cashel* and later John Maxwell, Jimmy Shanks and John Bannerman from *The Old Manse*, Jock Cameron from *Moorpark* and *Gartincaber*, Jimmy White from *Braeval*, Alan MacDonald and Peter Graham from *Corrie Grennan* and Donald Smith, the chief crocker, went round all the farms helping each other with the sheep work and when you think of the area that these farms covered, *The Old Manse* alone is about 1500 hectares, they were all needed, each one with two or three working collies, to gather in the sheep. This would be repeated again for the hogg clipping and marking in June when the lambs would be marked, in our case, with a fork on the left ear – the farm's own distinctive mark, the milk clipping in July when all the ewes were hand sheared, the speaning in September when the lambs went to market and for the Winter dip in November before the tups went out.

The pet lamb.   *Photo: Chrissie Bannerman*

The lamb sales were a traumatic time every year because the pet lambs had to go as well. These were the orphan lambs which had been hand reared all summer. This was a job for the children. It was their responsibility to bottle-feed the lambs, exciting at first till the novelty wore off and the regular feeding became a chore. But when it came time to part with them there were always tears and on occasions the pets mysteriously disappeared only to just as mysteriously reappear once the lorry had left for the market.

Mary Bannerman in the wool bag.
Photo: Chrissie Bannerman

The milk clipping - when all the ewes were sheared - although extremely hard work, was a great social occasion. Our milk clipping usually lasted three days between the gathering and the work at the fank. And the children had their own part to play. The apprenticeship started early for both the boys, Seonaidh and Gilbert, and the girls, Kate and Mary. The first job they got to do was the tarring. This involved running with a small pail of tar and a stick when they got a call from one of the shearers to disinfect any small nick that a ewe had suffered from the shears. They would also pick up any small clumps of wool that were lying around on the ground – the dags – and put them in a separate bag. When the children were a wee bit heavier they were put into the wool bags which were suspended from a kind of gallowslike structure so that they could tramp down the wool.

Then they graduated to rolling the fleeces then to crocking – which meant taking the ewes from the holding pens to the shearers under Donald Smith's experienced eye– and finally to the top job - the shearing itself. I think Kate might have dropped out by the final stages.

Donald Cameron at the clipping.
Photo: Chrissie Bannerman

My cousin, Donald Cameron from North Uist who worked in Glasgow, would arrange to have a few days off and in the early evening, when their own day's work was done, neighbours would arrive, men like Willie Ronald from *Gartfairn* and Alec Stewart the local postman, carrying a pair of shears in order to lend a hand. And to those who had been bent over the ewes all day shearing, they were a welcome sight.

Of course none of this could go on without a plentiful supply of food, starting with tea in the morning, then lunch and again tea in the afternoon and plenty of juice and beer to quench the thirst on a warm summer's day, all taken over to the fank.

At the end of the day the bulging wool bags were stored in the shed awaiting collection by Cooper's lorry which would take them to the wool buyers in Alexandria and everyone, numbers varied between twelve and eighteen, arrived back at the house for an evening meal and a well-earned dram and best of all, the swapping of stories.

Evening meal and a dram at *The Old Manse* after the work is done.
Photo: Chrissie Bannerman

The calves were also sold at the market in Stirling in September and the suckled calf sale was always on the Monday of the September weekend which meant an outing for all the family. The children looked forward to it because they would meet many of their school friends there, the boys could buy a toy farm implement in the shop to add to their collection and then there would be a meal in the restaurant at the market, a rare treat in those days and also an opportunity to meet with other members of the farming scene.

Although we were not aware of the phenomenon at the time, the first signs of global warning manifested themselves in the early years of our tenancy when it became more and more difficult to get the corn harvested due to heavier rainfall till eventually we abandoned this type of fodder altogether and concentrated on hay for a time but even this became gradually more difficult to harvest and we switched to silage, although still making as much hay as the weather allows. However the weather was not the only deciding factor. The older ways of working were all very labour intensive and depended on neighbouring and also a rural population which enjoyed taking part in farming activities even if they were not directly involved in farming themselves and the children's friends, especially Seonaidh's, would gather to help load and unload tractors just for the crack.

A hay field on *The Old Manse*. Left to right, Kate (on the tractor), Gilbert, John Proctor. Seated are Elizabeth Shanks, Sheila and John. *Photo: Chrissie Bannerman*

Inevitably the rural economy was changing. Farm incomes were falling and as a result sheep were coming off the hills and the shepherds with them. There were no longer enough people on the farms and even not enough farms as afforestation took over, to continue neighbouring. The quad bike took the place of the foot shepherd, the shepherds' cottages became holiday homes and agricultural contractors and machine shearing took over from the resident farm worker.

Many of the social activities suffered also although the Buchanan Sheepdog Society continues to flourish if not the Sheepdog Dance! The annual Buchanan Sheepdog Trials still attract a large entry of the élite of dog handlers. For many years the Trial was held in the *Arrochymore* field on *The Old Manse* with the local ladies being invited in turn to present the prizes to the successful participants and since it was a long day, with frequent visits to the tea-tent, the ladies had to be prepared to accept a fair number of exuberant kisses from the prize winners. When the trial was over, there was always a wee ceilidh in the tea-tent which the local ladies had manned (!) and for which they had provided the excellent food. Happily the Buchanan Sheepdog Trial continues although the venue has changed. It is now held at *Creityhall* but the competition is as strong as ever and the tea-tent continues to provide food and sustenance for all who attend.

Sheepdog trials at *The Old Manse*, 1992. Standing, L to R, Dochie McArthur, Iain Davie, Mary Bannerman, Rosie Allan, Liz Shanks, Katrina McAllister, Sheena McAllister, John McDougall, John Maxwell, Peter Graham, Jimmy McAdam, Robin Blair, John Bannerman, Ralph Wolfe, Geordie Turner. Seated, L to R, Walter McAllister, Jock Cameron, Jimmy Shanks, James Shanks. Jimmy Shanks is holding a trophy presented to him on retiring as Secretary of the Buchanan Sheepdog Society. *Photo: Willie Simpson*

The old way: Jimmy Shanks at *The Old Manse, 1970s.*
Photo: Willie Simpson

The new way: Robert Phillips and the late John Mailer, late 1980s
Photo: Chrissie Bannerman

Jimmy Shanks continued to manage the farm and latterly to train our daughter Mary to succeed him at the same time as she attended the Agricultural College at Auchencruive. She had always wanted to be a farmer. When she went to the Careers' Advice meeting at School she spoke to the representative from Auchencruive. He told her that attending Auchencruive would be a good career move because most of the girls who took the course ended up marrying farmers. Mary, in her usual blunt fashion informed him that she did not want to be a farmer's wife. The representative told her, "You have the wrong idea of a farmer's wife. They're not all big fat women with their hands in the flour bowl". (How PC was that?) Mary informed him, "I know. My mum is one and she's not fat! But I don't want to be a farmer's wife, I want to be the farmer." So when Jimmy retired he was so proud to hand over the reins to Mary. Sadly her stewardship was tragically cut short and Gilbert, who was at Auchencruive at the time, gave up his course and came home to take over. Young as he was, with his father to guide him and with the generous advice of our friends and neighbours, Walter McAllister and John MacDougall, the Duke's shepherds, he has kept the farm going as a commercial enterprise along with Sheila his extremely able and hard-working partner.

We still have a flock of Scottish Blackface sheep on the hills above Loch Lomond but we have replaced the cross cows with a fold of pedigree Highland Cattle in an effort to maintain a traditional farming enterprise which is as environmentally friendly as possible while at the same time being economically viable. We are fortunate to live and work in one of the most beautiful landscapes in Scotland. In late spring we hear the heartening sound of the cuckoo, all summer the whins glow golden on the slopes behind the house, Loch Lomond is ours to enjoy in all its moods and we are conscious that we have a duty to conserve this beauty for future generations as our forefathers did before us, but we are also well aware that without our work and our efforts, this place could very easily become a wilderness and that we most certainly do not want. We want to share it with all who want to enjoy it but only if they also accept responsibility for its care and its preservation. To them the old Gaelic greeting - Fàilte agus Furan - a warm welcome.

Gathering the Blackface at *The Old Manse*.   *Photo: Chrissie Bannerman*

Chrissie's mini suggests late 1960s. Two Canadian cousins (rear left), Lady Bannerman, Chrissie, Mary, Kate and John with Seonaidh.
Photo: Chrissie Bannerman

Jimmy Shanks and Chrissie, 1992.
Photo: Chrissie Bannerman

Lady Bannerman, John and dram at the Drymen Show. *Photo: Willie Simpson*

Left to right, Janice Stewart, Libby MacIntosh, Kate Bannerman, Marion Anderson; singing at a Mod in the late 1960s.   *Photo: Chrissie Bannerman*

Kate, Seonaidh and Mary, about 1970.   *Photo: Chrissie Bannerman*

Seonaidh and his daffs, Chrissie, Mary, Kate and wee Gilbert, 1975.
Photo: Chrissie Bannerman

John at the end of the day, about 1975.   *Photo: Willie Simpson*

Buchanan Portraits
Willie Simpson

Bill Brennan

Andy Donaldson

Mary Donaldson

Martin Pringle

Patricia Findlay

Willie Ronald

Donald McDermott

Annie Cameron

Calum Gow

Fred Perryman

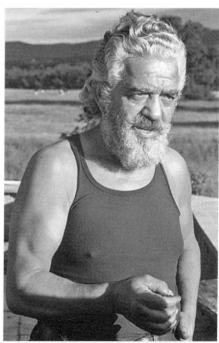

Oscar Catani

Bob Ferguson

Jessie McLaren

Sammy Stewart

Jock McCallum

The Music of Buchanan
Fiona MacMillan

Photo: Willie Simpson

Buchanan Parish has for long been an active centre of Scottish traditional music. Fiona MacMillan, now of *Coille Mhor*, spent the early years of her married life at *Dubh Loch Cottage*, and composed a march called *Dubh Loch Cottage* as she was scrubbing the kitchen floor. It has become a very popular tune with ceilidh bands all over Scotland and beyond. Fiona wrote the tune in the key of F. "It just came into my head one day," she says, "and down it went on paper." *Dubh Loch Cottage* appears in a book of Scottish Dance Music compiled by Iain Peterson and published in 1989 by Shian Music

Dubh Loch, Christmas 2002.   *Photo: James Taggart*

17

Dubh Loch Cottage   *March*   **by Fiona MacMillan**

Fiona's Jiggers. Fiona MacMillan ran a Ceilidh Dance class in the Memorial Hall over the winter of 2005-06. Left to right: Vivienne, Jean, Fiona, Audrey, Barbara, Maggie, Betty, Joe.   *Photo: Fiona Crooks*

Dochie McCallum was born 75 years ago in Dubh Loch Cottage, Rowardennan. His, father, grandfather and great-grandfather were all shepherds on Ben Lomond. For many years Dochie, who now lives in Buchanan Smithy, was the local postie. He is a weel kent and accomplished button accordion player. In 2005 he was awarded 'Best newcomer of the year' for his CD '*Naethin' Ower Fancy*'. (www.birnamcd.com). In 2006 he was awarded 'Guest artist of the year' for his performances with Neil MacMillan. On the next page is the tune Dochie wrote for Sheena, Neil's eldest daughter.

Dochie's CD cover.   *Photo: Fiona MacMillan*

Miss Sheena MacMillan of 'Coille mhor Cottage'

By Duncan McCallum 10/5/92

Janet MacMillan brought up her family of six children at the *Dubh Loch,* and that's where the young Neil learned to play the accordion, double bass and keyboards. He has written a beautiful Gaelic waltz for his mother, a Gaelic speaker herself, originally from Islay. This tune is also in Iain Peterson's collection, published by Shian Music. Neil says that very few musicians are able to interpret Gaelic waltzes properly, but it's easy for him since his father, also a Gaelic speaker, sang them around the house all through his childhood.

Mistress Janet MacMillan   *Waltz*   **by Neil MacMillan**

Neil with his Hohner Gola accordion.   *Photo: James Taggart*

A musical evening in the Memorial Hall to celebrate Dochie McCallum's 70th birthday.
Photo: Fiona MacMillan

Joel Milner of *Woodburn Cottage* pipes out the old Millennium at the *Dubh Loch*, 31st December 1999. On the right, Duncan Maxwell of *Blairvockie*.
Photo: Jenny Taggart

James Taggart of the *Dubh Loch* pipes in the new Millennium at *Blairvockie Farm*, 1st January 2000.
Photo: Willie Simpson

The University in Buchanan
Joe Twaddle

Joe Twaddle and his family lived at the University Field Station at Rowardennan for six years from 1966 to 1972. He left to work at Auchencruive in Ayr and the family lived in Kilmarnock. After a year he enrolled at Jordanhill College for teacher training and started at Balfron High Scholl teaching Biology – for twelve years. Meanwhile, after living in Balfron, they moved to Drymen in 1975 and finally to Balmaha in 1977. He taught in Dunblane High for a further thirteen years before retiring and taking up landscape gardening.

Photo: Jenny Taggart

The start of freshwater studies for students began in 1938 when Dr Harry Slack began a field course which then, after interruption by the War, resumed in 1946. This was organised from Balmaha and later transferred to Rossdhu on the west side of Loch Lomond. The site was provided by Sir Ivor Colquhoun of Luss, with some funding from Sir Harold Bowden. It became a focus for extensive research on Loch Lomond and its catchment. Of those involved before the move to the present site Jim Hamilton and Peter Maitland are best known to me.

In 1964 the present site at Ross Point was obtained from the Forestry Commission and new building erected. Harry and Flora Slack were prominent in the development of the facilities, and the first technician was John Flanagan who went to work in Canada in 1966. In June of that year Betty, Kevin and I arrived to an idyllic situation. We were warmly welcomed into a thriving community since close co-operation had been established with local people.

Dr and Mrs Slack rented *Blairvockie*, Nan Gow and Anne Bennett worked as cleaners and Jimmy Johnston was the handyman. At the time the houses at Sallochy were part of the Forestry Commission so there was lots of contact between there and the Field Station with Tom and May Fraser helping to keep a watchful eye on everyone and a young John Gow becoming an integral part of Field Station life.

Original Field Station at Rossdhu, about 1950.   *Photo: Joe Twaddle*

There were lots of community events - as there still are. At that time there was still a Buchanan Drama Society with Chrissie Bannerman the driving force and Rowardennan Hotel was the focal point. There were Burns Suppers with a couthy speech from Alick Macfarlane and songs from John Bannerman - both memorable. There were dances too, one in particular to celebrate Johnny Galbraith's retrial from the Forestry. It was great, but at the end an argument developed in the car park. We had an old Morris Traveller with a dud battery, so we couldn't get started. As usual no one would let you down so everyone broke off to give us a push. Fine! As we drove off on a lovely moonlit night I looked back in the rear mirror. Nothing had changed; the fracas had restarted where it left off.

The Field Station has two functions: to run field courses for undergraduate students and to provide research facilities. As well as Glasgow University students, there were courses from St Andrews (David Scott), Keele (Molly Badcock) and Hull. There was always lots of excitement when courses were running – mainly due to the fact that our amazing handyman, Jimmy Johnston, was also in charge of catering since he ran the Passfoot Tearoom with his wife Molly. It was great fun when these courses were there and even more so when Molly Johnston came to check that all was running smoothly.

There was even a time, in March 1970, when a big snowfall closed the Pass at Balmaha and we had to bring the meals up with the catamaran from Balmaha. Passfoot Tearoom was a popular place to visit and sample Jimmy's fish teas plus his special – spam fritters.

Betty and Joe Twaddle with Kevin, on the *Fiona*, about 1967.   *Photo: Joe Twaddle*

The research aspect of the Field Station involved several PhD students in residence plus Roger Tippet who arrived from Bristol in 1967. The first students were Pat Hamilton, Robert Russell, Forbes McNaughton, Jack Jackson and Walter Edger. Dr Tony Dixon also played and important role in establishing terrestrial research.

Over the years the personnel changed: Jim Bennett was technician, followed by Willie Gilmour and Liz Brodie. Ruby Doyle joined when ill health forced Anne Bennett to retire. New students were George Dunn, David Glenn, Steve Wratten, Keenan Smart, Mohamed Shafi and Baharam who was Kurdish. Jimmy was invaluable in nurturing the last two foreign students and giving them insights into Scottish culture.

Our two girls, Shona and Kirsty, were born during this time and since Kirsty was born at the Field Station, our memories of our stay there are particularly poignant. The romantic setting led to two weddings there – Liz and David Glenn plus Claire and Steve Wratten. This was our first experience of Rev Miller at Liz's wedding - one we will always remember. Steve's wedding was equally memorable as we tried to teach his family the intricacies of Scottish dancing in the big dormitory at the Field Station.

Jimmy Johnston, about 1968.   *Photo Joe Twaddle*

In 1972 Dr Slack retired and moved to Kilmarnock. Roger Tippet became director and Rab McMath took over my job. The Field Station continued to thrive and was extended in 1979 with a partnership between the Universities of Glasgow and Stirling.

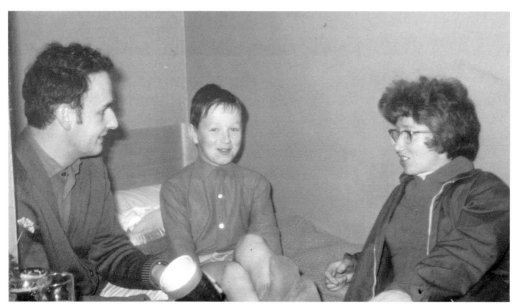

Roger Tippet, John Gow and Nan Gow, about 1968.   *Photo: Joe Twaddle*

Now even greater changes are occurring with Colin Adams in charge. The house where Kirsty was born has been replaced with an ultra efficient new building for research and staff accommodation, completed in October 2006. Funds are being put in place for a mirror image of the new building on the footprint of the existing accommodation and laboratory. This will provide a world-class centre which may benefit the community enormously.

We found that we missed the community so much that we were determined to get back as soon as we could and after several stages on the way we moved into Passfoot Cottage in Balmaha in 1978.

Part of the new Field Station, 2006.   *Photo: Joe Twaddle*

The Field Station from the air, with Dubh Lochan above, and Dubh Loch Cottage, 2006.
Photo: Joe Twaddle

Buchanan Countryside
Alasdair Eckersall

In 2001 Alasdair Eckersall moved to Rowardennan to take up the position of Ben Lomond Ranger for the National Trust for Scotland. He has been very active in this job, increasing awareness of the Ben Lomond environment through a series of organised rambles for locals and tourists, and helping to improve the environment by a massive programme of path renovation, path building, and rhododendron eradication, all using contracted labour and voluntary workers. He lives at Ardess *with wife Helen and children Connor, Catherine and Fergus.*

Photo: Helen Eckersall

Buchanan extends along almost the entire eastern shore of Loch Lomond, and reaches over the watershed of the hills above. This large area takes in a hugely varied landscape, supporting a large diversity of habitats and wildlife.

In altitude, the lands of Buchanan start just above sea level at the Lochside, where the nutrient enriched muds of Balmaha marshes provide for an abundance of aquatic and marsh plants, with a thriving food chain supporting insect, bird, fish and mammal life. The highest point is on the summit of Ben Lomond, at 974m altitude, where the harsh conditions mean only the hardiest, low growing plants can survive, including mosses, sedges, and the Dwarf Willow (*Salix herbaceae*), remnants of the tundra type vegetation which first re-colonised the glacier wasted surrounds of the Loch 11,000 years ago.

The landscape of Buchanan is very much a legacy of the glacial periods, but greater forces have left their mark too. The Highland Boundary Fault marks the dramatic meeting of two very different land masses, and crosses Buchanan in the ridge formed by the heights of Gualann, Conich Hill, and the island of Inchcailleach. When travelling the road up the east Lochside, the change in the land is very evident north of the Pass of Balmaha, the only road access across the fault line. The land to the south is much flatter and more given over to good pasture, the more fertile soils derived from sedimentary bedrocks. To the north the land is much hillier, and increasingly steep and rocky towards the northern end of the Loch, due to the greater resistance to glacial action of the ancient schist bedrocks.

Coire Corraly, Ben Lomond; woodland and willow scrub.   *Photo: Alasdair Eckersall*

Beyond Rowardennan, the glaciers scoured out a trough which plunges steeply down to a depth of 190m below sea level, to make Loch Lomond the third deepest loch in Scotland at this point. The hill slopes here are steep with thin peaty soils covering the bedrock higher up. Lower down the slopes a natural woodland cover dominated by oak and hazel managed to build up over time, amongst the jumble of rock outcrops and boulder fields. From *Ardess*, at the foot of Ben Lomond, southwards, the more gentle slopes hold deposits of moraine material pushed down by the glaciers, and this gave rise to a mosaic of heathy ridges, richer wooded areas, wet bogs and flushes.

Fragments of these older, natural habitats still survive in steeper gullies and wetter places, however most of the lower ground has been greatly changed, with constant use of the land by countless generations since the first human settlers in the area. Large parts are now given over to pasture grazing and forestry plantations of spruce, larch and pine. One of Loch Lomond's great assets though is the extent of oak dominated woodland. This is a legacy of past management to produce bark for tannin, as well as timber, but these woodlands, being no longer managed, are slowly reverting back to a more natural habitat. A developing under-story of holly, hazel and other native species combine to support an abundant variety of wildlife. Badger, roe and fallow deer, pine marten and feral goat are all present, and birds such as redstart, garden warbler and pied flycatcher attest to the growing richness of the woodlands as a habitat.

Feral goats above Rowardennan, 1998. *Photo: Alasdair Eckersall*

These woodland areas are expanding, as spruce plantations are harvested and replanted with native species, and as areas of rough grazing are planted with trees.

Adder by Ardess Wood, 1995. *Photo: Alasdair Eckersall*

Further up in the corries and on the high ground, thick blanket peats are dominated by dwarf shrubs including heather, blaeberry, and cross leaved heath. Drier heaths have been modified by decades of sheep grazing, giving rise to extensive slopes dominated by species-poor grassland.

Three members of the grouse family all occupy their niches here; black grouse on the mid-slopes on the upper woodland fringes, red grouse on the heaths and bogs, and ptarmigan on the summit moss heath of Ben Lomond. The steep base-rich crags on Ben Lomond still hold a rich variety of alpine flora, despite the attentions of nineteenth century plant collectors. The mountain is also home to the most southerly Scottish colony of the small mountain ringlet butterfly.

Juvenile ptarmigan on Ben Lomond, September 1998.   *Photo: Alasdair Eckersall*

These few brief mentions only give a taste of the range of habitat and wildlife to be found in Buchanan, but there is no doubt that with the range in landscape from Lochside to mountain top and major geological faults, nature has wrought us a richly varied place in which to live.

Small Mountain Ringlet butterfly. *Photo: Alasdair Eckersall*

Mossy Campion, on the slopes of Ben Lomond. *Photo: Alasdair Eckersall*

Carly and Lauren Bannerman
Rowardennan

Carly　　　　　*Photo: Michelle Frier*

Lauren　　　　　*Photo: Michelle Frier*

The Bannerman twins were born in Luton and brought up in Buchanan along with younger brother John by parents Michelle and Seonaidh. They are now students in Glasgow. Carly is studying graphic design at Metropolitan College and Lauren is studying Fashion and Management at Caledonian University.

Now being nineteen years old, sharing a flat with Carly, my twin sister, in Glasgow and attending University, I look back on my Buchanan years with fond memories. Buchanan Primary School was a small rural school where we all knew each other and it was far less intimidating than attending a larger school. As all of my father's side of the family lived in the same village, it was a huge comfort knowing there were friendly faces - whether it be family or close friends - to turn to for support.

Looking back on my school days it makes me happy but sad at the same time, on one hand thinking that obviously I will never have those fantastic years again and on the other hand thinking of the great times I had at Primary. Because it was such a close-knit community, I am still good friends with many of the people I went to school with and we often reminisce about our school days. We remember the games we used to play in the playground. The favourite was 'Bulldogs' which, when I was in Primary 4, I thought was

33

the best game ever as I got to play with the big ones and when the teacher banned it for being too aggressive I thought my life was over! I do remember vividly competing noisily with my sister to see who could finish our work first driving everyone else in the class crazy and annoying Mrs Norden. Being a twin in a very small primary school it was perhaps easier to have an individual identity but a struggle to avoid being tarred with the same brush. How lucky we were to have been brought up in such a friendly place and to have so many happy memories and good friends from there.

Rowardennan, where I grew up, is part of the Parish of Buchanan. It is an extremely small village, if you can even call it a village and it is possibly the hardest place to describe to anyone. Getting out of Rowardennan was also very hard as there is no public transport and you have a ten mile drive if you want to catch a bus from Drymen. The good thing about living in Rowardennan was that we did not have any neighbours and consequently no noise and we could make as much noise as we wanted which was normally quite a lot from our house, very different to living in a second floor flat in Glasgow with my sister Lauren where every move we make is heard by up-stairs and down-stairs – not good at three o'clock in the morning. Another advantage, I mean disadvantage, of living in Rowardennan was that when it snowed there was no way the school bus was going to make it up the road to get us.

One of mine and Lauren's fond memories of Buchanan is Sunday School and the Sunday School Trip to Inchcailleach. You would have thought by our excitement that we were off to a tropical island, but no, it was just across the water. When we were young it was the most exciting thing in our events calendar. We got to travel on the mail boat, swim in the water, go for walks over the island and enjoy a great Bar-B-Q prepared by the teachers.

To Sunday School with Alison Shanks.
Photo: Chrissie Bannerman

By the end of the day we would have sand everywhere, I would have probably lost my shoes and have a towel wrapped round me. Unfortunately we would then have to leave and they would have to peel us off the island unless it was raining and then we would happily step on the boat.

Lauren, Sunday School picnic, Port Bàn, Inchcalleach, 1997.
Photo: Chrissie Bannerman

Another social event we enjoyed very much was the Rural Christmas Party to which every child in the Parish was invited. We played all the party games and Santa Claus came and gave us all presents and the older ones tried to guess whether Santa Claus was Duncan MacFadyen or Gavin Shanks. The Rural ladies gave us a superb tea and on the way out we all got a tangerine.

We had looked forward for years to be old enough to go to the Youth Club because we heard such fantastic stories about it but unfortunately by the time we got there the good times were over and we don't really remember much about it. It stopped.

I am sure that everyone who attended Buchanan Primary School will agree that it was the best days of our lives and has equipped us to be absolutely useless in the big real world. Living in Glasgow as we do now, Lauren and I have come to realise that unlike Buchanan, you can't just walk around saying "Hi" to everyone as you'll probably get mugged or followed home. However Buchanan has introduced me to the best friends I will ever make and who will definitely be in my life forever whether they like it or not. Growing up in such a small community has its downside as moving away was made harder by always having been surrounded by people you had known all your life. However it has also made our lives more exciting as my first day at College proved. I had never been in a situation like it, of not being able to just chat away to anyone or everyone who would listen and that is what made it different and exhilarating. I had to meet people from all over the country and it is hard to explain to them where Buchanan and Rowardennan is, I had to remember that these people did not just live down the road or had known me since I could walk.

Carly and Lauren Bannerman

Becoming 'a big one' at Buchanan School was quite a big deal as we got to rule the school - or so we thought. During my time at Primary we did a lot of school productions, but my favourite one was *Charlie and The Chocolate Factory* which I played a lead role in. Obviously I turned down the main part of Willie Wonka and gave it to Aileen Saunders, as I felt my talents would be better used portraying Mrs. Salt alongside my sister Lauren who was Mr. Salt.

Carly, guess where and when?   *Photo: Chrissie Bannerman*

High School was a big scary move for us at the end of Primary where we had been used to a small class with only girls in it so in a way it was exciting to see what boys our age looked like. Unfortunately they were not that exciting when we met them. High School was particularly scary for me and Lauren as we were put into separate classes for the first time but I was also quite glad to be getting away from my twin. However having to do things by myself without anyone I knew being around and having to make my way round a massive high school full of big people was very scary in the end. Although at the time Balfron High seemed like the biggest school ever, now I am in Glasgow and at College it doesn't seem that bad and is even pretty small compared to the High Schools many of my new friends attended. The best thing about going to High School was going from travelling on the mini bus to going on the big bus which was also called the 'Bally bus'. On the 'Bally bus' we fought with the big ones about how far up we sat on the bus, oh and God forbid we sat up the back. Our lives would not be worth living. But I'm sure when I became a big one myself I was just as bad, if not worse because one of the wee ones was my wee brother John. I had a good time shouting at them.

When I was young I started my working career at Cashel Campsite helping out behind the counter. It wasn't a very high profile job but I got to eat as much as I wanted and messed the tills up a lot, but as my mum and dad were the bosses it wasn't a sackable offence. However they were quick to encourage me go to work at The Oak Tree Inn in Balmaha, where I spent four loyal years. The Oak Tree was my first real summer job that expanded into a winter, a night and a four year experience. Being only fourteen years old it was a bit daunting having responsibility for looking after other people and taking their food orders but I managed it - just.

The Oak Tree Inn, Balmaha. *Photo: Jenny Taggart*

I was one of the first people within my group of friends to get a summer job at The Oak Tree but soon there was a tribe of us. After I started, three of my friends joined me and already working there were some of my older friends so it was more a sociable place rather than a place of work. My dad called it 'the youth club'. The pay wasn't bad and I was able to afford my taxi up and down the road. But spending all my money getting to work did not seem so bad because it was like I was spending it hanging out with my friends anyway. During my days at The Oak Tree I did have some bad days, hating the customers, the chefs and Aggie for making me stay an extra five hours a day. To begin with I would have done anything not to go home, preferring to stay with my friends at work but when I reached eighteen I just was not excited about doing ten hour days in the summer. In the summer sometimes the pressure got a bit much and you would find some of the staff hiding in the corridors eating sandwiches and drinking cans of Red Bull because the place was too busy to get a break. Other pressures within The Oak Tree were keeping the chefs happy. If there was so much as a wrong order given to the kitchen all hell would break loose and all day there would be a constant war between the superior, I must say, waiting staff and the kitchen staff. It would continue sometimes into your lunch because if you had really annoyed the kitchen you would get tabasco in your tuna and cucumber sandwich - not pleasant. The other people who wouldn't be happy with wrong orders were the customers. I mean it's not my fault if I didn't hear you say you wanted an arctic charr which takes thirty minutes to cook and now everyone else is eating but you. This happened quite a lot to me because of my writing which also aggravated the kitchen. Apart from that I considered myself to be a fantastic waitress and I'm sure so did my bosses and the many people who had to carry me, I mean work alongside me, all those happy, busy years.

Like Carly, my first job consisted of totally messing up the Cashel Campsite tills and fighting over who got to work behind the counter. However at other times it was the total opposite because of the nice summer days and the Loch only a skip away - where we spent all our summers. After Cashel I went on to bigger and better things in Drymen. When I was fourteen, I started my first proper part-time job at The Pottery. Fortunately Peter - the owner - was a friend of my dad's which helped me to avoid an interview and worked hugely to getting the job. However I knew it was actually due to my fantastic waitressing skills which he had spotted whilst I served him his roll and egg at the Campsite. I went on to work for four long, happy years with Peter and I was thrown into every area of The Pottery, one day I would be a café waitress and the next I would be in the kitchen showing the chefs how to cook. By the end of my time in The Pottery I was serving up pints of Best and putting up with rowdy Drymeners and grumpy old men who pointed out every little mistake I made when serving them.

The Pottery, Drymen.   *Photo: Jenny Taggart*

Throughout my time at The Pottery there was many an eventful day filled with moaning customers, as the scones were too hard or complaining of a draught - whilst sitting next to a cosy warm fire. Also colleagues who had been working together far too long resulting in no one getting served and the odd fight. The only down side of working in The Pottery is my size as I'm still paying for the numerous slices of chocolate cake consumed on a daily basis - sorry Peter! I very much enjoyed working in The Pottery and was extremely nervous when I had to enter the 'real' world where an interview for a job was normal. Now when I go back to visit they tell me they miss me terribly and I usually have to take my own order which is actually more than I did when I worked there.

Being brought up in Buchanan was a fantastic experience for us both. We have wonderful memories and wonderful friends from there. Although we enjoy Glasgow we also realise how fortunate we are to have to have lived in Buchanan surrounded by a close and supportive community and our home is still there.

Arthur Bayfield
Buchanan Castle

Arthur Bayfield is head greenkeeper at Buchanan Castle Golf Club, as was his father before him. His family has long and deep connections with the sport locally. One of his sons, Stuart, is a greenkeeper at the Loch Lomond Golf Club; the other, David, is with the RAF. He lives with his wife Jean in Buchanan Castle Estate.

Photo: Arthur Bayfield

My paternal grandfather came up from Norfolk to work for the fifth Duke of Montrose in 1920. My dad was then five years old. My maternal grandparents were from Yoker in Glasgow. My grandfather was a shipwright. Mum and dad met when dad worked on Buchanan Castle Golf Course and mum worked in the clubhouse. They married in 1940. Mum was evacuated to Cheltenham to her sister's during the war and my sister Alice was born there in 1942. I was born in Yoker in 1946. Mum and dad started their married life in one of the flats at Buchanan Stables and when I was six months old we went to live in one of the new council houses at Buchanan Smithy – No. 9.

Ten new houses had been built beside the Montrose Estates houses of the 1870s. My sister Jean was born there and still lives there with her husband. Times were hard for parents at that time but growing up at Buchanan Smithy was a joy, roaming all over the woods and fields without a care in the world.

In the field behind the houses we played football, cricket, golf, sledging in the fields in winter. Was there more snow then? It was the old story, everyone knew you and you knew everyone. I still remember the people who lived in these houses:-

No. 1   Peter and Tina Cameron
No. 2   Jimmie and Anne Vickers, Jim, Jeanetta and Catrina

No. 3	Bill and Lou Maitland and son Fergus
No. 4	Mrs Johnson and son Willie
No. 5	Davie and Beanie Ross
No. 6	Alex and Betty Stewart and daughter Janice
No. 7	Jock and Jessie McCallum and nephew Duncan
No. 8	Mary McNaughton and daughter Catharine
No. 9	Arthur and Mary Bayfield, Alice, Arthur and Jean
No.10	Tommy and Francis Anderson, Gillian and Marion.

School was slightly different then than now. Buchanan School was in the house across from the present school and the headmaster stayed in the house to its left – looking from the present school. Teachers were Miss Ewan and Miss Macfarlane. When I think of what we played - down the burn even when it was in spate, down The Mains field, going through the Sawmill (where Duncan and Kathleen MacFadyen live now). We had our sport's days there and we played up around the back of the church – no health and safety then.

I remember the small classrooms with lovely stoves - can't remember whether the stoves were oil-fired or wood burning - suffice to say we never seemed to be cold in winter. Talking of winter, we used to pour water down the playground the night before and the next morning we had a fantastic slide. The head teacher's house held the library and primary 7 children were the librarians for the school on a Friday afternoon, this being reading time. Sitting reading in a very quiet schoolroom with the sun streaming through the windows was a lovely time. Then you would see Jock's bus arrive to take some of the children home to Rowardennan and then you knew it was time to go home. Not so good was when you saw the dreaded White Van. This was the school doctor or dentist. You sat shaking in your shoes waiting for your turn.

School dinners were made on site by Betty Forbes (Sandy's mum) and they were great. We walked home. Sometimes, when it was nice, we meandered, stopping to play with the melting tar on the road, or if you were in a hurry you would run between some telegraph poles and walk between others. Nearing Halloween you would pick a turnip out of one of the Duke's fields. If you were really lucky Jock McCallum or Tom Ronald or someone would give you a lift home in their car or van or lorry.

Members of my generation will remember the SWRI Christmas parties. They were held in the Tearoom at Balmaha then they moved to the Memorial Hall, Milton of Buchanan. I wonder who Santa was?

One of my happy memories is when the call would go up, "Duncan MacFadyen is home". At that time Duncan worked all over the world and when he came home you wondered what he had brought with him. One year it was a motorbike, another year a Ford Mustang sports car and one year, for goodness sake, it was an aeroplane. He used to land it in The Mains field and even today when I walk past the site I wonder how on earth did he ever manage that.

After primary it was off to Balfron High School – not as good fun as primary but bearable. What a difference the new High School has made. It was a good school in my day, but now it is consistently in the top echelon in Scotland.

When older, I had a summer job helping Jock McCallum. Jock had a haulage business. You name it - he hauled it - logs, coal, gravel. I remember hauling gravel from

Milarrochy Bay to the sheep fank at *The Old Manse*. Jock's nephew Duncan and I helped Jock to load the lorry using shovels. No mechanical diggers then. One of Jock's contracts was to collect the rubbish bins in the area - high-sided lorry and heavy metal bins full of ash – say no more. The rubbish was dumped at the old quarry on Buchanan Castle Estate.

Jock's lorries were kept at Buchanan Smithy. The row of houses on the Balmaha side of The Smithy were derelict and some had just frontage left – the lorries were kept behind them. Now fifty years later they have all been rebuilt and are homes again.

A young Stuart Bayfield on a flooded course   *Photo: Willie Simpson*

After school I could not decide what to do. My uncle lived in Corby and worked in the steel mill, so I went down to see if I could get an apprenticeship. Can you imaging going from somewhere like Buchanan to a steel town? I hated it. I lasted a year and that was because of the kindness of my aunt and uncle. At that time my father, who worked on the golf course, said they were looking someone to help on the course. I jumped at the chance. That would do until something better came along. That was forty-three years ago. So, at the age of sixteen and three quarters, in 1963, I joined my father on Buchanan Castle Golf Course under Head Greenkeeper Bill Bradford.

Arthur Bayfield senior, an expert with the switch   *Photo: Willie Simpson*

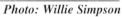

A tribute to two generations of Bayfields   *Photo: Willie Simpson*

Arthur Bayfield

Bill Bradford was ahead of his time. He, and one or two others, started a Scottish Greenkeepers' Association, which started in the West of Scotland and has evolved over the years to the present British and International Golf Greenkeepers' Association. He was also instrumental in starting a greenkeepers' apprenticeship scheme and I was the third person to be taken on under this scheme. I was given a good grounding in greenkeeping by a tough, but kindly Bill Bradford. He died in 1969 but his daughter Isobel Waddell still lives beside the golf clubhouse.

My father, Arthur senior, became Head Greenkeeper until he retired in 1979 when I took over. There have been only three Head Greenkeepers in seventy years. When the golf course was built in 1936 it was extremely long and difficult, and during the Second World War it was shortened to what you see now. I don't remember the course before it was shortened but if you wander through some of the fields beside the present 14th/15th fairways, and know where to look in parts of the rough, you get a very good idea of what it must have been like; likewise the *Castle*. I don't remember it anything other than a ruin. When the roof was removed in 1954 I was seven, but listening to my parents and earlier my paternal grandfather, my aunts and uncles, it must have quite a sight in its heyday.

Arthur Sr.   *Photo: Arthur Bayfield*

Arthur Jr.   *Photo: Arthur Bayfield*

In 1973 I married Jean whom I met through a golfing friend. We started our married life in Buchanan Stables down below where my parents had begun their life together. In

Arthur Bayfield

1977 our son David was born and in 1979 second son Stuart. When Stuart was six months old I became Head Greenkeeper and we moved down to *The Bungalow* where we remain to this day.

Both boys attended Buchanan Primary School and Balfron High School. David is now a sergeant in the RAF. He is an air loadmaster on Chinook helicopters, and as such he has visited many parts of the world – some parts perhaps his mum and I wished he hadn't! Stuart is a third generation greenkeeper and went to the prestigious Loch Lomond Golf Course for his work experience from school and when he left school they took him on, originally for an apprenticeship. He has been there nine years.

The Bayfield family have had a long connection to Strathendrick Golf Club – Buchanan Castle's older brother – created in 1901. I have been a member man and boy for many years as was my father and grandfather and both my sons. Most of the trophies have a Bayfield name on them. Recently Stuart won a trophy which dated back to the 1920s. On four occasions it had been won by his great grandfather. I myself have been fortunate enough to win Strathendrick Club Championship on four occasions.

This is briefly my living history of the parish of Buchanan. My elder sister died a few years ago but my younger sister still lives at Buchanan Smithy. The parish grips you and although I am the most non-committee minded person, I have done two stints on the committee of Strathendrick Golf Course. I am presently on the Buchanan School Board, the school my father, aunts, uncles, sisters and sons went to. I am the worst gardener in the world but I am on the Flower Show Committee and on the Memorial Hall Committee. I am also involved in the life of the Church. The Church was always there but Jean was a churchgoer and when the boys started Sunday School I began going along. I joined the Church and later became an Elder and am now Session Clerk.

The parish of Buchanan has always been community minded and friendly. This is still the case today. Names may change but the ethos remains the same.

The Flower Show.   *Photo: Willie Simpson*

Buchanan Schoolchildren, 2007

Buchanan School, 2007.   *Photo: James Taggart*

David, age 8

I like living in Buchanan because it is quiet and not too many traffic problems. I like going for walks up the Conich and going to the park. I like to see the sheep and the horse called Billy. I like the view of the country. I like the summer when I go up to the farm and see the lambs and you get to feed them.

Amber, age 11

My favourite things are the school, the view, the area and the houses. I like the school because it is small and you get to know everyone in it. I love the view of the Conich in the morning, it makes a lovely shadow. The area is very small but very open. The fields make it calm and settling. I especially like the houses because they are all together. My favourite house is the farm house up at Creityhall Road. I also love the wildlife like the baby lambs with the sheep, the sheep dogs and the great hawk.

Buchanan Schoolchildren

Lauren, age 11

I love Milton of Buchanan because it is quiet, small and clean and no loud traffic at early hours in the morning. We have a great park surrounded by cows, calves and sheep in the fields that separate houses. I can go for a walk with my friend up Creityhall Road. The views are amazing! (like Conich Hill). Children can ride their bikes without worrying about vehicles.

We have beautiful flowers especially the snowdrops. We have a big church and a Memorial Hall, which in summer clubs go on in it. Most of all it is a great place to grow up in! I wouldn't prefer anywhere else to stay!

Nathaniel, age 10

I like Buchanan because there is no vandalism around. I also like Buchanan because it is a safe and small place to grow up in. I also like the nature and all the country smells. It is a VERY good place to grow up in because at night there are no teenagers shouting and smashing bottles on the ground. Also at night no loud cars come through playing music very loudly. It is also a safe place to ride your bike.

Jessica, age 8

I like Milton of Buchanan because it is quiet. It is nice to ride your bike and it is a good place to grow up. It has got lots of snowdrops, it is safe and small and not too many traffic problems.

Buchanan schoolchildren from a by-gone time.   *Photo: Sandy Fraser*

Annie Cameron
Buchanan Smithy

Annie Cameron is 87 and enjoys good health. She has two daughters. Elizabeth was born in The Stables in Buchanan Castle, and now lives in Drymen. Myra lives in the Western Isles. Annie has five grandchildren and nine great-grandchildren.

Photo: Jenny Taggart

In April 1941 I came to Buchanan to work from Gartocharn with two friends, sisters Jean and Jenny Patrick, to be interviewed for the post of working land girls by Mr Glen, the then factor for Montrose Estates. This resulted in all three of us being employed at Buchanan Home Farm, known then as Ibert Farm, which was part of Montrose Estates. It was a dairy farm, which carried a large herd of Ayrshire cattle and some horses that were required for fieldwork as many crops were grown at that time. They were supplemented by two tractors and the appropriate machinery where necessary.

Employed on the farm were the grieve (foreman), Mr Bill Fraser, head ploughman John Boyd, dairyman Joe Bland plus several extra workers, as required. Henry and Marie Melville lived in the gardener's cottage behind which was a long corrugated iron building, which housed three dormitories, a small kitchen and an outside WC. This became our home while we worked there, in my case for about a year. The reason for that was I met my future husband Hugh Cameron who worked with Montrose Estates at that time and for many years later. We married and moved to another house within the Home Farm.

Our main work was in the fields, except in midsummer, when we were dispatched to operate a large grass-drying machine, which contained three large drying trays. One of the girls filled a tray with newly cut grass from the nearby golf course. This, in turn, was transferred to other trays until the drying process was complete. From there the grass was forked into a small bale, the resulting bales being then stacked in a large shed for winter feeding.

The present Duke's grandfather, the Sixth Duke of Montrose, took special interest in the drying machine because, as far as I can remember, it was the only one in the whole district.

Rudolf Hess   *Photo: Internet*

Buchanan Castle had become a military hospital during those war years and I can remember the patients who were able to walk through the farm on their way to Drymen village, stopping to watch us working the machine. They would sometimes stand for a considerable time, quite fascinated by the whole operation. The hospital's most notorious patient then was the Nazi leader Rudolph Hess who had been taken there after his mysterious flight from Germany to Scotland. One evening we went to our drying green to hang some washing and were suddenly surrounded by soldiers, who it turned out were guards policing the area while Hess was at the hospital. I have vivid memories of their rifles pointing at us while they questioned us concerning our reason for being there.

Every Saturday night a dance was held at Crow's Tearoom, now the Winnock Hotel, in Drymen village. This was very well attended and provided a social occasion for those of us who worked all the rest of the week. The Crow family eventually emigrated to New Zealand and the Tearoom changed hands.

As the years passed each land girl got married and left to live their new lives. I have continued to live in Buchanan since then, moving eventually to Buchanan Smithy from our flat at The Stables, near the golf clubhouse.

I am proud to be part of Buchanan community and have many happy memories of life in the area stretching back sixty years to those days at the Home Farm.

Carol Cameron
Gartincaber

Carol Cameron (Sellar) is married to Ronnie, a local haulage contractor. Her home is on the Gartocharn Road, almost directly across the River Endrick from where she was born at Milton of Buchanan. Carol and Ronnie have three children: Lindsay who lives in Glasgow, Ross who lives in Fiji, and Kirsty who lives in Vancouver.

Photo: Jenny Taggart

I was born on 16 September 1947 at *Gartincaber Cottage* and was the middle child of Albert and Jean Sellar. My father was employed by the 7th Duke of Montrose as chauffeur and gardener at *Auchmar*, or the *Big House* as we used to call it. My mother also worked there as a housekeeper. *Auchmar* employed a lot of staff then: a butler, cooks, housemaids and at least two gardeners.

My father's chauffeur job gave him the opportunity to drive a beautiful Bentley car and whilst parked outside, my sister and I took a chance to sit in the back and marvel at all the comforts for first class journeys. And being the head gardener, there were always a few perks, one of them being access to the surplus garden and greenhouse produce.

Wages were low then, so ways to economise had to be found. My mother would sew and knit a lot of our clothes. She used to say we were some of the best-dressed children in Buchanan. Looking back at old photographs, I have serious doubts at times! We really did live off the land in those days. We never went hungry, there was always fruit and veg from our garden and we kept chickens for eggs and the occasional roast dinner. My father would shoot rabbits, ducks and pigeons and there was always the odd pheasant or salmon found it's way into our kitchen.

Carol Cameron

I can remember not having electricity for a time with only the Tilley lamp and candles for light and the Baxi coal and log fire for cooking and baking. Mum was a good cook and baker. It was all simple and wholesome food. Delicious.

Our milk had to be collected from Minnie Ronald at the Milton Farm in a metal milk can and it was my job to collect it. My biggest fear was getting past the tied up collies which were usually asleep until they spied me, when they would leap up barking furiously and run towards me. Many a time I came home without any milk.

We very rarely ventured out of Buchanan as we didn't have a car and we had to rely on the infrequent services of McKinley's bus to take us to the bigger village of Drymen. A big treat on a Friday was a chocolate biscuit each when my mother went to Drymen for her messages. We did have delivery vans throughout the week calling at the cottage: the baker, the butcher and the grocer's van. It all had to be paid in cash then.

Gartincaber Farm was a working farm which required manual labour. Adjoining the cottage was a one room kitchen, bathroom and living space called the *Bothy* that was used by the Duke to accommodate any short-term workers on the Estate. Periodically, it was used as accommodation for local young couples. Billy and Anne Anderson, Peter and Ann Johnson and George and Jean Cummine were our neighbours for a time.

Gartincaber Cottage with the Bothy on the right.   *Photo: Carol Cameron*

Carol Cameron

Harvest time was always a busy time on the farm and the more hands the better. As children, we didn't do very much work, but we joined in so we could get a ride on the horse and cart to and from the fields. Great fun!

There was a week in October when the children had a holiday from school for the tattie picking. It was back breaking work, but a few pennies in your pocket made it all worthwhile. Mrs Miller, the farmer's wife, was a welcome sight as she strode across the field with a large tea urn in one hand and a basket of homemade bread and jam sandwiches in the other. The farm butter was not one of my favourite tastes, but we were always hungry and grateful for a sit down. Health and hygiene never came into it as we got stuck in with our earth-encrusted fingers.

When I was at Buchanan School it was across the road from where the school is now. It had two classrooms. In the first few years Miss Macfarlane taught the children and then they moved into Miss Ewan's class until they went to the High School at Balfron.

Miss Ewan lived next door in the Schoolhouse and I can still see her marching back after lunch with her dustcoat flapping in her wake. She was very strict, but kind. I got the belt only once when I foolishly went along with a prank to place a tack on one of my classmate's chairs - Arthur Bayfield, John Cowie, Alice McIntyre, Ann Benny, Ronnie McLaren and the victim Alan Savage, to name a few.

I remember I always went home for lunch, the main meal of the day - soup, meat and pudding. We were all round the table. My father had walked down from *Auchmar* through the glen, my brother Albert would cycle home from his job at Norrie Baird's market garden at Balmaha, and my sister Jean, who was four years my junior.

Sisters Carol (left) and Jean Sellar, 1956/7.   *Photo: Carol Cameron*

The Milton was where I met up with local children to play the usual ball games etc. and Mrs Dugdale was always a force to be reckoned with when we had to ask for our ball back.

A rare trip to Glasgow; Albert Sellar with young Albert and Carol, 1951.
Photo: Carol Cameron

Carol, age 3. *Photo: Carol Cameron*

We had to make our own entertainment then and I spent a large part of my summer time on the Mar Burn which was full of special places to play house, have picnics, catch baggie minnows and navigate across the burn on the large boulders on stones which were very visible when the burn was low. When it was in spate after a lot of rain, it sounded like thunder as it crashed its way down to the River Endrick. The salmon came up in the late autumn to spawn and we had great fun trying to catch one as it battled its way upstream. We were never very successful though.

In the winter the cottage had to be heated with coal fires and my father spent his spare time collecting and sawing wood to fuel them. The living room was the warmest room, so most of our evening activities were there. We would play cards and board games, whilst listening to the radio. We also played darts on the back of the living room door - the holes for the stray darts looked like we had been infested with woodworm.

Sunday was always a day for donning our best clothes and going to Church or Sunday School. Mr Fulton was the minister then. The Sunday School was taken in the Memorial Hall and I can still see those stuffed birds and animals that lined the walls in glass cases around the room, which was called The Museum. There were also a variety of bird's eggs and various artefacts.

Carol Cameron

The Memorial Hall was the place for social activities: whist drive, carpet bowls, WRI meetings, dances, drama productions and of course, the Annual Buchanan Flower Show. It was always a big event. For weeks before the show my mother would knit, sew and bake and my father would the garden to produce his best.

Andy Donaldson always won the cup. His attention to his garden paid off. I can remember seeing his chrysanthemums over the garden wall with the bags over their heads to protect the blooms from wind, rain and early frosts.

During the summer, we would have trips to Balmaha. With picnic in hand we would cross the wooden walkway across from the shop and garage owned by Duncan McLean, to the Boatyard, climb over the dyke and go around to the shallows to paddle. You could walk quite far out and the water would still be below your knees. It was very safe and sandy. If you wanted to hike up to Manse Bay it was deeper for swimming. We would sometimes hire a rowing boat from Alick Macfarlane, but never got very far out of the bay.

A special trip would be the *Maid of the Loch* steamer from the pier - a sail to the top of the Loch and back. Going below deck we would watch the large engines pumping the paddles around. I can still smell the oil used to keep them running smoothly.

Bicycles were used a lot as a way of getting around, the roads being a good deal quieter then. It was always a second-hand bike for me. The back yard was usually littered with bits of cycle and motorbike parts to be used as spares. The homemade go-kart was always a favourite for bombing down the farm road.

As I grew into my teens, Jean Cummine, née Ronald, who had moved down from Rowardennan to Creityhall Drive, became a close friend. We spent our time between her house and mine, doing the usual teenage stuff - listening to the hits of the 60s, gossiping about local boys and latest fashions, going for long walks and cycle runs, going to local dances, meeting up with the local boys, and through time, marrying them.

Ronnie Cameron (left) and George Cummine at *Langwell*, Croftamie, 1962.
Photo: Carol Cameron

Carol Cameron

We were members of the local drama group. It was great fun, but the actual performances were nerve-racking. I remember being on the big stage in the production of *Highland Wedding*. I was playing the bride and George Cummine was the groom. I felt so embarrassed when I had to kiss him on stage.

There were no streetlights in those days and the road to *Gartincaber* could be pitch dark. Jean and I would escort each other to the halfway point which was Buchanan Church. During the war German soldiers had been buried in the churchyard and I can remember when they were taking the coffins back home to Germany to be buried. I would have to walk past the open graves to get home. I didn't hang around. Making haste up the farm road in the complete darkness, I ran headlong into big Jimmy Smith who had been visiting my brother. I don't know who got the biggest fright.

There was a working sawmill in Buchanan at that time which gave employment to about ten people. The Cowies, the McIntyres, the Rosses and the Reids all lived on the premises in the wooden houses. Some people had to take an extra job to increase their income and my father and mother got employment at Shalloch Farm from the Biggart family. In that kind of employment friendships developed over the years and still continue to this day.

Time moved on, places closed down and people moved away and I was one of them, but when I look back on these precious years spent in Buchanan I feel privileged to have grown up in that place and at that time.

Cast of *The Highland Wedding*, 1961. Back row, left to right: George Cummine, Mr Sinclair (teacher at Buchanan), Mrs Sinclair, Neil Cairns, Peter MacMillan, John Macfarlane, Alex Stokes. Front row: Nancy Ronald, Jean Ronald, Carol Sellar, Fiona Cairns, Mary Donaldson.   *Photo: Carol Cameron*

Flora Cameron
Milton of Buchanan

Flora Cameron is now 87 years old. Originally from Glasgow, she has lived locally since she was twenty. She has been in her present home in Milton of Buchanan for fifty-eight years. She enjoys life and likes to keep busy. She is now a great-grandmother, with another great-grand child expected this year.

Photo: Jenny Taggart

My name is, Flora Cameron. I was born and brought up in Glasgow, one of nine children. I came to Balmaha in 1940 expecting to work as a land girl but when I arrived was told I was not needed.

Montrose House was being prepared to be used as a rest home for munitions workers. It was run by The Union of Girls Clubs. The Warden heard that I was not needed as a land girl and offered me a job at *Montrose House*. My wage was 16s a week with full board. The cook was Betty Forbes. She lived at *Passfoot Cottage*. We became good friends and I learnt a lot from her. The munitions workers came for weekends for 3s6d or a week's full board for 21s. We had about thirty girls staying each week.

I used to cycle into Glasgow every week on my day off to see my family. I wish I could still do that!

I was a founder member of Buchanan SWRI when it started on 29th January 1942. I wasn't married then and my name was Flora Reid. It was held in the school. We opened with a Burns Supper and had a great time. The President was Mrs Lacey the Minister's wife. We met once a month. I learnt a great deal from all the demonstrations we saw and I entered as many competitions as I could. We had great fun presenting shows and pantomimes to local groups.

Flora Cameron

We used to can all our home-grown fruit. We were able to use *Montrose House* for this and I got up very early to light the fire under the boiler to have it ready for the WRI members to can their fruit. The cans cost 5d each. It is very sad that the WRI finished in the village in 2005.

The Annual Buchanan Flower Show started in 1946 and is still held on the last Saturday in August. Competition is fierce in all categories: Fruit, Flowers and Vegetables and Rural Industries. My name can be found engraved on most of the trophies which are presented

I worked at *Montrose House* for five years. When the war was over I went to work for the Minister, Mr Fulton, at *The Manse* (now known as *Shalloch*).

Munitions workers dancing on the lawn at Montrose House.   *Photo: Flora Cameron*

There was no electricity, therefore I had to maintain and light all the oil lamps and there was a large range fire and a four-burner oil cooker in the kitchen, which I also maintained. In fact, I made my own wedding cake baking it in that oil cooker, borrowing ration coupons from everyone.

Flora Cameron

Flora Cameron at home. *Photo: Willie Simpson*

I was working at *The Manse* in 1947 the year of the very bad winter, which made life very difficult for everyone. The Loch froze over and we all went ice-skating on it and it was great fun, although probably very dangerous.

I got married in 1948 to Mr Ian (Jock) Cameron. At that time he worked at Gartfairn Farm but soon started to work at Gartincaber for the Duke of Montrose where he stayed until his retirement. Ian's father was gamekeeper to the family at *Ptarmigan* (north of Rowardennan Youth Hostel) and Ian attended Sallochy School.

When the new houses were planned at The Milton I applied for one, only telling Ian about it when I knew we had been allocated one in June 1949. We moved into the house I still live in on 9th September 1949. I continued to work at *The Manse*, cycling each way every day.

On the 20th October my first baby, Helen, decided to arrive a month early (perhaps it was the cycling) She was the first baby to be born in the new houses at The Milton. My son Hughie, born four years later was the first boy. We had a very happy time as they grew up, growing all our own fruit and vegetable in the garden across the road.

During our early years at The Milton, from our upstairs windows, we had a lovely view of the Loch and could see the steamer the *Maid of the Loch* coming across from Balloch to the pier at Balmaha. Unfortunately trees were planted and grew very quickly to spoil our view. The Forestry trees have recently been cut down but sadly the beech hedge in front of the planted trees has been allowed to grow into tall trees and so our view is still blocked. I would really love to be able to see the Loch and the Dumpling Hill at Gartocharn from my bedroom windows again.

The steamer carried locals and visitors up and down the Loch. When they disembarked from the steamer at Balmaha they were required to pay pier dues of 2d, collected by Mr John Macfarlane. He was related to Mr Alick Macfarlane who owned the Boatyard at Balmaha and delivered the mail to the houses on the islands on the Loch, a tradition still carried on by his descendants to-day.

During this time I worked for Professor Glaister at *The Cluan* for about thirteen years and when Mr Galbraith acquired the house I worked for him for a further eighteen years until my husband Ian had his stroke. I also worked for a time at the Tearoom at Balmaha until unfortunately it burnt down.

When Ian retired from work the neighbours arranged a party for him in Drymen. We knew nothing about it until we arrived. It was a great surprise. Sadly, shortly after retiring Ian suffered a stroke, I cared for him for eight and a half years until I had a heart attack and was unable to nurse him any longer. He was in *Dalnair House* at Croftamie for two and a half years until his death.

My daughter and son both married and had their own families. Helen, living in Croftamie, has two sons, Donald and Alasdair. Donald is married to Louise and they live in Buchanan Castle Estate. Hughie lives in Cambusbarron and has one son, Alan. He is married and has a son, Ethan, so I am now a great grandmother.

I am less able to get out and about now but still enjoy trips out with Helen and my neighbour Glennys Nichols who was the District Nurse. She helped me care for Ian and then looked after me (and still does). Trips out for lunch, going round Garden Centres and enjoying the scenery are very enjoyable.

I really miss not being able to swim any longer I have always loved it and for several years was a member of the Buchanan Club at the Buchanan Arms, although I had to give up two years ago.

I manage with a little help to grow tomatoes in the greenhouse and also do a little gardening. The children next door help by filling the water barrels for me. I also continue to enjoy knitting and still do some baking when I can.

I have had a very happy life here at The Milton and I thank God for it every day. The Milton has certainly changed in recent years; the only original tenants still here are Mr Angus MacFadyen and Mrs Jeanetta Doherty and myself.

Flora worked at the Balmaha Tearoom.   *Photo: Willie Simpson*

Jimmy Coubrough
Balmaha

In 1990, Jimmy Coubrough returned from Canada to his native Scotland. He lived in a caravan, behind the original Ben Lomond Cottage *at Rowardennan, owned at the time by Jock McLaren, the roadman. He worked for Balmaha-based Sandy Fraser Electrical Contractors. Jimmy then moved to* Glendorian Cottage, *known locally as* The Kentucky Hut, *situated on the Stirling Road, on the outskirts of Drymen. Now, due to failing eyesight, he lives in sheltered accommodation in Alexandria.*

Photo: Jenny Taggart

I was born in Alexandria. I have a long history of family connections with the Buchanan area. My paternal grandmother was Jean MacDougall of *Arrochybeg*. I have this memento of her:

> Arrochymore, Arrochyleck, Arrochybeg, Milarrochy
> Three miles up the Pass, then you come to Sallochy
> Past Critreoch and The Blair
> Where Patey Mertin shot the hare.

The first two lines of this rhyme were handed down in my family from Jean MacDougall of *Arrochybeg*, and the last part from my aunt's friend, a Miss Macfarlane of *Arrochyleck*. It was a children's rhyme recited as they went to Sallochy School in the late 1800s.

I have researched my family back as far as the 1830s. I am related to the McIntyres, MacDougalls and McLarens - all local families. Grandmother Jean MacDougall married David Coubrough from Clachan of Campsie. She left the area to live with her new husband on a Killearn farm, and later moved to Jamestown in the Vale of Leven. Her sister married into the Veitch family, who were saddlers to the Duke.

Jimmy Coubrough

When I was sixteen years I emigrated with my older sister and her husband to Canada where I became an electrician. I lived for many years in Vancouver, returning to Rowardennan in 1990, when I was 54. I always say "old age brought me home!"

First I lived in a caravan, behind the original *Ben Lomond Cottage* at Rowardennan, owned at the time by Jock McLaren, the roadman. I worked for Sandy Fraser Electrical Contractors down at Balmaha. Later, I went to stay in *Glendorian Cottage*, known locally as the *Kentucky Hut*, situated on the Stirling Road just up from Fraser Robb's outside Drymen. I am now seventy years and because of poor eyesight I live in sheltered accommodation in Alexandria.

Although I lived a long time in Canada, I can speak fluent Gaelic. I had childhood memories of active Gaelic societies in the Vale of Leven in the late 1940s and very early 1950s, and as a child I knew a little Gaelic. This inspired me to learn the language. I also became a good piper. You can read about me in the books. But I can't play now as I have arthritis in my fingers.

Jock McLaren, roadman, Balmaha.   *Photo: Willie Simpson*

Lily Cowie
Milton of Buchanan

Lily and Jack Cowie came to Buchanan in 1950. Lily is a native of Tarland in Aberdeenshire, and still speaks broad Aberdeen. She is 83 and has three children – Isobel, John and Douglas. She now lives in Muthill, Perthshire near her family.

In 1950 my late husband Jack, myself and our young family arrived at Milton of Buchanan where my husband had got work at the Sawmill. We were complete strangers but in no time we were over whelmed by the kindness and generosity of the people of Buchanan, who until this day have kept up true friendships. Sadly lots of good friends have passed away. There were the Johnsons, MacFadyens, McIntyres, Grays and Ronalds and many more, plus the workers of the Sawmill, where my husband was foreman. He always had good reliable staff.

In 1953 a severe gale in the north of Scotland left thousands of acres of woodland flattened which meant all the workers had to be transported to near Aboyne on Deeside for a period of two years. Eventually we got back to our beloved Buchanan.

My young family enjoyed the Buchanan School until it was time to go for higher education at Balfron.

My late husband enjoyed fishing, Drama Club and other hobbies, mostly woodwork.

Jack Cowie with his children
Photo: Peter Johnson

Jack Cowie with his catch
Photo: Peter Johnson

I enjoyed SWRI meetings and our local church ministered by Rev F H Fulton, who is still alive, and Rev Ian Gray, sadly gone. My family also enjoyed Sunday School run by another friend, Mary Donaldson.

In the summer we had trips down the Clyde on the *Waverley* and *Jeanie Deans*. TV was coming into fashion, but for this my family depended on visits to the Maitlands at The Smiddy.

I have many more happy memories of Buchanan and Drymen and the good folk we will never forget.

Paddle Steamer *Waverley* on the Firth of Clyde.   *Photo: Internet*

Paddle Steamer *Jeannie Deans* approaching the Kyles of Bute.   *Photo: Internet*

Jean Cummine
Milton of Buchanan

Jean Cummine has lived in Buchanan all her life. She has been a stalwart of the WRI, the Flower Show, and is Joint Church Officer with husband George at Buchanan Kirk. For many years, Jean poured a mean cup of coffee in The Pottery at Drymen. Jean and George have two sons (Andrew and Mark) and a daughter (Linda). They also have six grandchildren and counting.

Photo: Jenny Taggart

My parents were John and Agnes Ronald. My older brother Ian and I were born in *Coille Mhor Cottage* where Neil and Fiona MacMillan now live. My first memory is aged three, standing in the front of Jock McCallum's tipper lorry moving house to *Lomond Cottage* and being told to get back from the windscreen in case I bumped my head. Mum had the sideboard clock wrapped in a towel for safety on her knee. *Lomond Cottage* was great; it had a flushing toilet, a novelty which kept me occupied all day while the adults got on with bringing in the furniture. My father worked for the Collins family who owned most of Rowardennan at that time, and mum helped in their house which is now the Youth Hostel.

When the Forestry Commission took over my father was given a job with them and mum worked in the Rowardennan Hotel and for the Russell-Ferguson family who lived at *Sallochy*.

As children, summers were spent at the burn, the Loch or climbing the hills. Our aunt from Motherwell was convinced we would either drown or break our necks falling down the hill. At weekends we had to be in clean clothes, sandshoes whitened to go and meet the *Maid of the Loch* at Rowardennan Pier just in case visitors arrived, which they often did.

Rowardennan Youth Hostel, formerly home to the Collins family. *Photo: James Taggart*

The Youth Hostel was another playground where we taught ourselves to ride bicycles up the drive keeping near the grass edge so that we had a soft landing.

Carbide gas was used to light the Hostel, and one day dad was supposed to keep an eye on me while doing a job at the outhouse where the used carbide came out into a tank. Left alone for a minute I climbed onto the edge of the tank to walk around the rim. I, of course, fell in. It was deeper than I thought. Surfacing now and then I could hear dad calling my name, eventually finding me and running home carrying me over his shoulder, getting me washed down. Panic over.

Parties in the Common Room at the Hostel were great fun, the children all doing a party piece and being greatly praised by the adults. In winter we still climbed the hills looking for the high icicles which hung down from the rocks. They could have done a lot of damage if they had fallen on us with their long sharp points. We were, of course, forbidden to go near them.

When there was snow and ice on The Ben and lower hills, the wild goats came down to the field in front of the house. One of them ran at me every morning as I walked to the Hotel to get the school bus. I was running rings round my brother screaming, while being told to stand still, which I never did. Mum appeared with a stick and herded the goat away. After a few days I was told the men had taken the goat on the ferry and set it free on the other side of the Loch. Confidently I set off for school - the goat was back. Mum

Feral billy goat at Rowardennan.   *Photo: Internet*

and her stick saw us past the goats every morning until they went back to higher ground. Tom Kerr owned the Hotel and the school bus and Dochie McLaren drove us to school from the Hotel. He also worked in and around the Hotel and drove the ferry across the Loch in the summer time.

Dochie, his wife Lizzie and their two daughters lived in a cottage behind the Hotel and Lizzie worked in the Hotel. As there were few telephones in Rowardennan, any urgent messages were left at the Hotel and Lizzie walked up to the house to pass them on.

The McCallum family lived at *The Cluan*; Cathy and I spent a lot of time at each other's homes, walking there and back unless an older brother gave us a lift on the crossbar of his bike. We were good at amusing ourselves and disappeared for hours until we were hungry and lots of home baking filled us up.

In 1953 our family moved to *Woodburn Cottage*, by which time Cathy and her family had moved to stay in Drymen, so I was Billy-no-mate for a while.

However, in 1956 the MacMillan family came to stay in *Dubh Loch Cottage*. I now had five children to entertain me. Jan and I being nearest in ages, we spent our time walking between *Woodburn* and *Dubh Loch* or keeping an eye on the younger MacMillans when asked to.

Going away for a weekend was not for the faint-hearted. In winter we got a lift to Buchanan School, always on a Friday so I got the day off, then we walked to Drymen, usually missing the Glasgow bus. Not far out of Drymen we would get a lift in a milk tanker into Balloch where we would get a bus to Glasgow and on to Motherwell. On the way home: bus to Drymen, walk to Buchanan, miss the school bus, walk home. "How far now?" was the cry. "Not much further, just up this hill and round the next corner" was the reply. There were a lot of hills and corners before we reached *Woodburn*.

Ronnie Cameron and George Cummine, 1957.   *Photo: Jean Cummine*

While living at *Woodburn*, Ian left school and began to work in Glasgow, which meant living with our relatives in Motherwell as travelling home each day was not possible. I started at Balfron High School and enjoyed my time there, again transported by Dochie McLaren to Balmaha and on to Balfron by bus.

When I was thirteen, the family came to live at Milton of Buchanan and Ian came home to live. Carol Sellar and I were pals, giggling teenagers, walking to each other's homes, and in summer to Balmaha. We met friends, including boys and both of us holiday jobs in the Winnock Hotel in Drymen.

The Dramatic Society in the Memorial Hall was fun way to pass the long winter's nights. Learning the lines and rehearsing was not taken too seriously but we enjoyed being in the plays as much as the audience enjoyed coming to see us.

Through time we both married local boys, me to George and Carol to Ronnie Cameron. We remain friends and still laugh at our earlier exploits.

In 1973 the McAllister family came to stay at Creityhall Farm and our children grew up together. They responded to a 'telling-off' from either set of parents and knew they come to any of our doors if they needed help.

Life in the Buchanan area is never dull and many people have asked what we do with ourselves in this quiet place. I never really had time to weary.

Teenagers Jean and Carol (on George Cummine's motor bike). *Photo: Jean Cummine*

Jean with John Macfarlane in a Dramatic Society production. *Photo: Jean Cummine*

Sandy Fraser
Balmaha

Sandy Fraser was born and brought up in Buchanan. He has worked here all his life and is a successful businessman, offering stable employment to his staff at Balmaha.
He is a passionate family man and a great supporter of all community activities in the Parish. Resident at Balmaha until recently, he now lives at Rowardennan with his wife Lucy and their children.

Photo: James Taggart

I was born at the Forestry houses at Rowardennan on 1ˢᵗ January 1955. I have two older brothers, Ian and Tom, and a younger stepbrother Graham.

My father, Tom, started as a forester in 1928 at Darnaway in Morayshire. In 1930 he became an assistant at Balmoral Castle. He joined the RAF at the beginning of the war and served as a rear gunner and radio operator. He survived being shot down in the Bay of Biscay. After the war he joined the Forestry Commission and after a short stay at Aberfoyle he was sent to Rowardennan as Head Forester, living firstly at *Woodburn Cottage* and then at *Dunmore* at the Forestry houses. He managed the area until he retired to *Arrochoile* in Balmaha in1971.

My mother, Maisey, died in 1958 when I was three years old and my father, after a succession of housekeepers, married May Perryman from Buchanan Castle. May's father and mother stayed in the north wing of Buchanan Castle and Fred, May's father was the electrician. His job was to look after the DC generator that was located beside the Castle. It also supplied the clubhouse with electricity. One of the stories he used to tell us was that he was working on the electrics in the building that Rudolph Hess was taken to for a short time and he overheard Hess trying to explain to two guards what he would like to eat. He was trying to pronounce something and my grandfather suggested that what he wanted was Scottish soup, which after some debating proved correct.

Tom Fraser Sr.   *Photo: Willie Simpson*

May Fraser.   *Photo: Willie Simpson*

In 1961 May, my stepmother, decided to start a Bed and Breakfast primarily because she needed our three-piece suite recovered. At that time she charged 12s9d. By 1982 she was charging £5.50p – she blamed that on high Council rates. In 1980 she was chosen to represent Scottish landladies in a promotional tour of America run by the Tourist Board. She was described on American television as the top B&B hostess in Britain.

My childhood memories are of fishing in the local burns for brown trout, playing football two or three a side until it got dark, and looking for Garvie's lemonade bottles that got you three pence as long as the lid was on – Cashel shop rules! You could also take them to Jackie Frier at Milarrochy Bay Campsite - he didn't look too closely.

My most frightening memory was the school bus overturning on the Cashel straight. Acid from the battery burnt my brother Tom and Hughie Glass. We had to climb out of the window and ran all the way home. Dochie McLaren, the driver, was standing outside swearing at the bus as we all climbed out.

I married Lucy Oliver in 1979. We had eight children, James, Stuart, David, Emma, Sandy Jnr., Krystina, Holly and Ben. We started married life in a caravan at *Arrochoile* then moved to *Hollybush* in Drymen for a short time. We then moved back to *Point Cottage* at Balmaha. In 1986 we built *Moniack* in Balmaha and then *Lomond Cottage* at Rowardennan in 1995 and finally The Oak Tree Inn, Balmaha, in 1997. I started Alexander Fraser Electrical Services in 1976, running the business from *Point Cottage* originally.

We tragically lost James in an accident in 1999. Stuart works as our head chef in The Oak Tree Inn and David is a director of Fraser Electrical. Emma is at University and Sandy Jnr. is training in The Oak Tree kitchen. Krystina is at college, Holly is at Balfron High School and Ben is at Buchanan Primary. We are delighted that our older children have decided to live and work on the east side of Loch Lomond.

Sandy's father and grandfather in Rowardennan forest.   *Photo: Sandy Fraser*

Sandy and Lucy Fraser with all their children.   *Photo: Lucy Fraser*

Nan Gow
Arrochybeg

Calum and Nan married in 1958 and lived at Forestry Cottages, Rowardennan with their son John for fifteen years. They moved to Creityhall Road, Milton of Buchanan and lived there for twenty-eight years. They now live in Charles Crescent in Drymen enjoying their retirement.

Photo: Jenny Taggart

My childhood days I spent at *Arrochybeg*. I came to *Arrochybeg* in 1939 with my father, John Galbraith, my mother and my brother Donald. My father worked for the late Lord Bannerman at the *Old Manse*. I was four years old and lived at *Arrochybeg* for seventeen years. I was educated at Buchanan Primary School and Balfron High. A school bus, owned by Mr Kerr of Rowardennan Hotel, took us to school. *Arrochybeg* had no electricity. We used paraffin Tilley lamps for lighting and my mother cooked and baked on an open range fire.

I used to go lambing with my father and helped feed the wee motherless lambs with cow's milk. I helped at the sheep clippings, rolling up the sheep's fleece after it was sheared. We had three horses to do all the arable work on the farm. No tractors in those days! It was my job to take them to a burn behind the house for a drink after a busy working day.

I had two pet goats, Rummy and Ludo. If they got into the house they would drink milk from a basin in the dairy and eat anything they could find. We called them the terrible twins.

Our yearly treat was a sail up the Loch on the steamer to have a picnic at Luss, Tarbet, Inversnaid or even Rowardennan. We had never seen Rowardennan. Very few people owned cars. We got lemonade at Mrs Johnson's shop at Passfoot on the way to the pier at Balmaha.

These are some of the memories of my happy days at *Arrochybeg*.

Arrochybeg, 2007   *Photo: James Taggart*

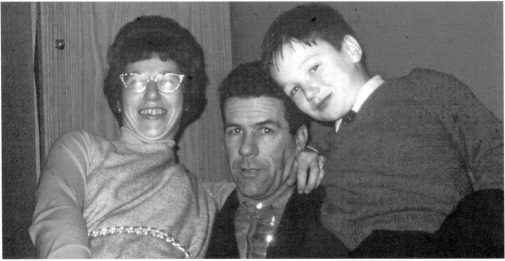

Nan, Calum and John Gow, about 1969.   *Photo: Joe Twaddle*

John Henry
Anchorage Cottage

From 1964, Anchorage Cottage, *Rowardennan was John Henry's holiday home. Recently, daughter Izzi and her husband Ivor rebuilt the Lochside house that they now run as a B&B. John is 87 years and still works most days either with his son at the family garage in Dalmuir, or helping at* Anchorage Cottage *especially in the summer months. He lives alone in Hardgate.*

Photo: Izzi Corbally

I purchased the *Anchorage Cottage* during 1964 for the princely sum of £1000. At that time it was a stone walled room, with a prefabricated extension added, which had been made at John Browns Shipbuilders, with no mains water or electricity, a chemical toilet and if you were caught short through the night hours you're only lighting inside the lavatory was provided by a candle. It's amazing how long you can put off a visit to the loo when it's dark and raining. The water we drank was from the burn. It also served as the fridge, and the milk was in the burn to keep cool. The burn was our wash hand basin with plenty of cold running water for the hardy visitors to the *Anchorage.* I had electricity installed fairly soon after purchasing the cottage. When mains water pipes were laid I had that installed too because during hot, sunny summers the burn almost ran dry. The cottage in its time has been a stable for the ponies working in the slate quarry on the hill above, a post office and also a wee shop.

I upgraded *Anchorage Cottage* during 1973, adding a kitchen and bathroom. The original kitchenette became a small bedroom for my son. My daughter Izzi and son-in-law Ivor Corbally demolished the old cottage during 1997 and had the existing building erected during 1998.

Over the years I have had the privilege of knowing many of the characters who lived along the Loch. Johnny Galbraith, who for many years lived and worked at Rowardennan, was a very good friend. His home was constructed with corrugated aluminum sheeting. His house was known by his friends as *Squirrel Bar*. I, like many others, have spent many happy hours sitting with Johnny enjoying a dram whilst listening to the resident mice running around inside the settee I was sitting on. On some occasions it was possible to hear the bottles in his sideboard jingling as the mice pushed past them. Sandy and Lucy Fraser have built a beautiful home, *Ben Lomond Cottage*, on the site now. Johnny was real character and is sadly missed by all who knew him.

When Johnny's daughter and son-in-law, Nan and Calum, lived in the Forestry Cottages at Sallochy, Nan managed to breed and rear capercaillies by hand. She's the only person I know who has done that. My family remember going out with Nan to collect caterpillars to feed them. I have fond memories of their time in both Sallochy and Milton of Buchanan. Our sons are great friends to this day. John Gow can be seen wearing out a pair of running shoes most nights between Drymen and Balmaha.

Annie and Jackie Frier lived in *Balmaha House* and ran a Bed & Breakfast business. Annie and Jackie had hearts of gold, made all welcome, and loved a dram with any visitor. They had an unusual clock on their wall which was given to them by the comedian Billy Connelly. The time was read as oneish past twoish and so on.

There are so many folk who I have had the privilege of knowing over the years. Laurie and Wilma Lilburn were friends for more years than I care to remember to both my late wife Jean and I. When Wilma lost her brave fight against cancer, Laurie was lucky enough to find happiness with Alice and recently moved to Killearn. Kevin, Laurie's son has now taken on the challenge of *Sallochy House* and its grounds.

Tom Fraser, Head Forester, ran the forest with firm hand - no fires or litter and woe betides any offender who did not respect the Loch. Alec and Doris Crawford who lived at Rowardennan. Thanks to Alec the trees that grew too big or were too close to the old *Anchorage Cottage* became firewood. Bill Brennan was the Warden at Cashel Camp site and still lives there to this day.

I recall Bob and Jean Nicol who owned and ran the Rowardennan Hotel, as well as many previous owners. I can remember when if you wanted to park your car in the Hotel car park on a Sunday evening it was best arrive early. The bar would be three deep waiting to be served. However, there where lots of accidents involving drunk drivers on the run home. Thankfully, folk have seen the error of their ways, apart from the boy racers who visit the area on occasion. I remember Johnny Galbraith calling into the Hotel bar not long before he moved from Rowardennan to live with Nan his daughter. "A bowl of soup and a half of whisky please," he whispered to the barman. "Mr Nichol lets me have that for a pound." Bob overheard him but ignored it, then whispered to me, smiling, "It costs me money when your pal comes in at lunch time".

Neil and Fiona MacMillan's New Year's parties are quite something, and all the locals attend. Great music and food, great evening - but beware of the measures Neil pours. After about an hour, Ivor thinks he's a musician - God help us. Duncan McCallum (Dochie), the accordionist from Buchanan Smithy, usually plays a few tunes at the party along with other stars of the Scottish dance music scene. He made a CD of his music during 2005; it's really great and well worth purchasing.

Dochie McCallum with his beloved button box
Photo: Willie Simpson

Angie MacFadyen, a friend for many years, launches my boat and helps me take it out at the end of the season. He is a true craftsman and the boats he has produced over the years are fine examples of just how a boat should be built. I look forward to his visits as he can help fill me in on what I have missed over the previous season.

There have been so many memorable days on the Loch, but the annual launching of the original *Anchorage Belle* is clearest in my mind. When I finally retire I might have more time to reminisce, but 87 is too young to stop work. I would miss the crack and if you sit at the fire for too long you get old very quickly.

For many years my late wife Jean went to visit her sister in Edinburgh at Easter, allowing me time to launch the *Anchorage Belle* along with my cronies, most of who have now gone to the Big Fishing Club in the Sky. Although I do know that Peter Holmes the gamekeeper and well-known dog breeder and trainer is doing well, as his wife Lois looks after my daughter's cat Minky when she goes on holiday.

John Henry

We would all arrive get the fire going and have a whisky or two, whilst we peeled the potatoes. These were boiled with salted herring sitting on top. You definitely require at least four or five chasers to wash down salted herring - a bottle did not survive for long in these days. Our plan was to launch the boat and whitewash the exterior of the old *Anchorage Cottage* after the winter weather. Most of this was achieved, as was the emptying of the bottles we brought. On completion there would be four or five white headed and white faced drunks to be returned to their families. I don't remember us catching any fish at Easter, I wonder why? We did however smell like one.

A good day's work. *Anchorage Belle* **in the background.**
Photo: John Henry

I also have fond memories of visiting my sister Margaret and brother-in-law Dougie MacDonald on the island of Inchfad where they lived and farmed for many years, only leaving during 1984 due to Dougie's ill health. Farming an island is hard work; for example, procuring winter feed for the stock was in itself a major operation. Feed had to be unloaded from a lorry at Balmaha, then moved onto the jetty. From the jetty it was loaded onto a barge, towed to the shore of Inchfad, unloaded, carried up to the farm trailer and again loaded and taken to the stack byre and unloaded again. Any tasks that involved goods being brought to the island had to be done in this way. Moving livestock to the mainland was also a hazardous venture. How many folk would wish to share a barge with an unhappy bull?

I know Dougie loved his time on the island, as did Margaret. Both missed it when they moved to Elgin on the doctor's advice. That part of Scotland is reputed to be better for anyone suffering from arthritis. Sadly Dougie died during 1999. Margaret now lives in Drymen. Dougie's son Graham lives with his family on a vineyard and olive grove in

New Zealand. The first wine named *Courage Creek* should be ready for distribution during 2007.

With my brother James, leaving Inchfad. *Photo: John Henry*

John Henry, sister Margaret and her husband Dougie with another fish on Inchfad.
Photo: John Henry

Peter Hunt
Blairvockie Farm

Peter Hunt emigrated to America in 1966. He worked as a graphic designer before becoming a serious artist in 1998. He married a 'yankee-doodle-dandy', Maryanne, in 1972. They have two boys: Colin, 32, is a full time painter and Ian, 30, is the bartender at the Nobu restaurant in NY. Peter and Maryanne live quietly in New Hope, Pennsylvania. Maryanne has a flower shop in Doylestown, Pennsylvania.

Photo: Peter Hunt

The Hunt family lived at *Blairvockie Farmhouse* from 1953 to about 1964. Father Fred drove to his office in Glasgow every day. He was General Manager of John Haig & Co. Pam was the receptionist at the Buchanan Arms Hotel in Drymen; her friend Gillian also worked there and lived nearby. Wendy was a stewardess with British European Airways. Mike was a salesman for Carreras cigarettes. He now lives in Perth, Western Australia with his wife Moyra Ferguson and family. Moyra was brought up on the Buchanan Castle Estate.

I was in the RAF doing National Service before going to Glasgow School of Art. I would come home to *Blairvockie* at the weekends. I am now a painter and live in Pennsylvania, USA.

Donald and Cathie MacLean lived in the cottage behind our house. Donald was awarded an MBE for his services to farming in Scotland, and now lives, I think, near Tyndrum.

My mother, Irene Hunt, enjoyed the company of Cathie MacDonald who lived next door in the shepherd's cottage. She and Cathie looked forward to the postie's visits. Because of our isolation his deliveries often included other essentials besides the mail. Donald Maclean's (not the shepherd Donald MacLean, see above) store in Balmaha was our closest shopping to buy a few basics such as milk and tinned food.

Lambing and sheep shearing were busy events on the farm. The dip was nearby our house and we all got involved. Donald McDermott, another local shepherd, lived in a cottage along the road towards Rowardennan. He and Donald MacLean (the shepherd) were good friends and worked together. On occasion they enjoyed the resources of the Rowardennan Hotel while they were gathering sheep. Their dogs maintained watch over the sheep outside the Hotel bar until it was time to go home.

We did not have electricity during the time we lived at *Blairvockie*; a Tilley lamp was required. Another form of lighting was provided by carbide gas acetylene generated in an outhouse. Donald attended the making of the gas by pouring water on the carbide under an inverted funnel to catch the gas. Drinking water was obtained from a damned stream some yards up the hill from the farm and piped down to our houses.

One of the most enjoyable aspects of living at *Blairvockie* was sailing on the Loch. We owned a 14-foot sailboat and a 12-foot rowing dingy with an old Seagull outboard engine. We kept both boats tied to trees at the water's edge, on the point across from Luss. The Loch is not tidal and made this kind of tie-up possible. On Sundays during the summer some of us would boat over to Luss for the Sunday papers.

A tame sheep named Deeta (so named because of her liking for Ryvita biscuits) was a family pet. She had been hand fed by Cathie when she was a lamb. Deeta maintained her ties with the flock, but she would come to you when called and separate herself from the flock in the hope of a biscuit, or she would come to the kitchen window in the mornings.

Blairvockie Farmhouse　　　　　　　　　　　　　　　*Photo: Willie Simpson*

The Islands of the Parish
John Macfarlane

Amongst the thirty or so islands of Loch Lomond, five are in Buchanan Parish; and only two of these, Inchfad and Inchcruin, have been inhabited in recent times. Both of these were formerly part of the Montrose Estates. Inchcruin was bought in the early 1920s by Mr Malcolm Irvine, and has remained as a holiday home for his descendants to this day. His granddaughter, Mrs Irene Paton, recalls that Mr Irvine was an early pioneer in the film industry, having been a co-founder of the company Scottish Films. The aim of Scottish Films was to 'put Scotland on the screen so that its history, its beauty and its life and industry can be seen in all corners of the world'.

Irvine invented the Albion Truphonic Sound System on which the company's talking pictures were recorded. Malcolm Irvine also invented a process for casehardening steel which was adopted by the growing motorcar industry. The photo (*courtesy, John Macfarlane*) shows Mr Irvine standing on the shore of his Island home.

Inchfad was bought from Montrose Estates in the 1940s by Frank and Anne Davison, a couple whose subsequent adventures led to tragedy, when Frank was drowned at sea during a sailing trip. The lives of Frank and Anne on Inchfad, and their sometimes-critical observations on the 'locals' are colourfully described in Anne's book *Home was an Island*.

After the Davisons left Inchfad to embark on their ill-fated ocean voyage, the island became home to a succession of families over the next ten years: the Mitchells, the Hewitts, and the McDonalds. Dougie McDonald and his wife Margaret are remembered for their success in restoring a certain level of productive farming to the island, and their family were sadly missed when they left the island in the 1980s.

Since then, Inchfad has in the main, been tenanted by caretaker occupants working on behalf of absentee landlords such as a Mr Ted Tolman who was involved in Richard Branson's record-breaking crossing of the Atlantic by speedboat. The island at present is owned by a Mr Harding, an industrialist based in Yorkshire, and is occupied by caretakers who look after the property including two houses, barns, jetties, boats and grounds.

Although the island has mains power (thanks to a cable laid from Balmaha in the 1950s), and telephone, the necessity to ferry everything by boat and the vagaries of gales, floods and ice must add to the challenges not to mention frustrations, of island life.

Dougie and Margaret McDonald meet the Mail Boat, Inchfad, about 1965.
Photo: John Macfarlane

Inchfad Jetty, completely icebound: March 1963   *Photo: John Macfarlane*

Peter Johnson
Milton of Buchanan

Born in 1934 at an Estate cottage in Milton of Buchanan, Peter Johnson has lived all his life, except for three years RAF service, in the village. His parents moved to Mar Achlais *in 1934 and this was his home until his marriage to Anne in 1958. After a short time at part of* Gartincaber Cottage *he and Anne moved to Creityhall Drive where their two children were born. The bulk of his working life was with publishers DC Thomson. He has three grandchildren and one sister.*

Photo: Jenny Taggart

On 24 July 1934 when I was born, my father was employed by Montrose Estates and was the occupant of a cottage supplied by the Estate, at Milton of Buchanan. It was one of four homes within the building at that time, although at a later date they were converted to two, as at present. The four families residing in the cottages then were the Finlays, MacFadyens, Johnsons and Campbells, all estate employees. Johnny Campbell was the local meal miller. A substantial area of ground on the other side of the road was divided into four gardens which were extensively used for growing vegetables, keeping hens and the storing of firewood etc. Each house also had an outhouse to the rear and at each end where livestock - probably pigs - had once been kept.

In 1937 when my father left the Estate to take up employment with Stirling County Council as roadman between Drymen and Balmaha, we moved into a new house which the Council had built for him. My father decided to name the house *Mar Achlais* because it was situated between those two burns. Interestingly when the house was sold by the Council in recent times, the new owners retained the name. The vacated cottage was then occupied by the Grays with daughter Margaret who would be little more than a year old. A wonderful spirit of trust and neighbourliness prevailed. There was no such thing as locked doors or fitted burglar alarms. Everyone helped and shared with each other as required, which was a great advantage when the Second World War broke out in 1939. As a consequence most of our early childhood was dominated by wartime activities.

An early memory is of being fitted with 'Mickey Mouse' gas masks which was looked upon as great fun. Of course we did not understand the seriousness of a gas attack or other aspects of impending danger and the fact that our parents must have been really apprehensive and worried didn't cross our minds.

Before my father was conscripted for service in the army, he carried out air-raid patrol duties around the area. One night he called at the house to point out the exploding bombs in the sky over Clydebank and lifting me above his head for a clearer view, I can remember the whole brightly lit scene.

In common with the rest of rural Britain several residents of Buchanan opened up their homes to evacuated children, mainly from the Glasgow area. They quickly adapted to their new surroundings making friends with the local children and happily starting school. My mother gave accommodation to the wife and two young daughters of a Royal Naval reserve officer who had been posted to Glasgow from England. This turned out to be a happy arrangement for both families while our respective fathers were away from home. The Bacons settled happily at Milton where they remained for the next four years taking a real interest in local life and helping enthusiastically with work concerning the war effort.

The Bacon family after the War. *Photo: Peter Johnson*

Buchanan Primary School roll practically doubled with the influx of evacuee children creating a great deal of extra work for the teachers. The school building was on the opposite side of the road from the present school. It was divided into two rooms known by the children as the 'wee room' (infants, classes 1 and 2) and the 'big room' which catered for classes 3, 4 and 5. At the gable end of each classroom a cheerful coal fire surrounded by a large guard burned during the winter months. Lighting was by gas lamps which were supplied by gas kept in a shed at the rear of the school building. Also at the rear were the toilets which necessitated the pupil having to ask permission of the teacher to go outside when the need to use them arose. Miss Johnston, who lived in Drymen, taught the early classes while the older pupils were the responsibility of head teacher Mrs Black who lived in the house beside the school. Both teachers were very gifted in the art of passing on knowledge, ensuring a good primary education for the child who was willing to learn. Before lessons the school day usually began with the singing of a children's hymn accompanied by the piano played by the teacher. Singing and music tuition were very much part of the curriculum, as were all the main Bible stories of the Old Testament and Gospels. The building opposite was at that time used as a general purposes room divided into two compartments by a sliding partition. The children were taken across there for physical training, visits from the district nurse or dental inspections, and for Christmas parties, when tables would be laid out with treats. This building was also used for some adult functions, including local dances, when the partition would be opened to accommodate the number of participants crowding into a rather restricted area.

In the back garden at *Mar Achlais*. Left to right, Margaret Gray, Peter Johnson, Margaret Bacon, Peter Smith holding Marion Johnson, Elizabeth Bacon. *Photo: Peter Johnson*

Leading through the wood was a track to The Mains field where the boys played football at lunch break. Poor Mrs Black. On many occasions she had to come right down the track blowing her whistle over and over again to summon the apparently unhearing pupils back to school for afternoon studies. The Mains field was also used for sports days when the children would cool off by paddling in the cool waters of the Mar Burn. Other activities were held in The Mains field over the years, such as football games with jackets placed on the ground for goalposts. One celebration which our generation will remember perhaps more than others was the bonfire and accompanying joy at the VE (Victory in Europe) party. A large crowd of locals gathered around the bonfire at the bottom end of the field before proceeding to the school hall for dancing and refreshments.

Wings for Victory parade at the Buchanan Memorial Hall.　　　*Photo: Peter Johnson*

The Buchanan Memorial Hall still contained a great many exhibits collected from various parts of the world which intrigued locals and visitors alike. Known as the Museum, it housed beautifully stuffed animals and birds, some in glass fronted compartments with the natural habitat in the background. Pull-out drawers full of bird egg collections were of much interest to the children, some of whom spent many hours looking in hedgerows, trees and moorland for nests containing eggs from which one would be taken for a proudly owned display at home. Across from the main hall door stood a corrugated iron construction known as the Playshed, which provided wonderful entertainment for the schoolchildren during breaks or on a wet day. A variety of games were played there, some of them involving rather too much rough and tumble. Near the Playshed stood a stone sculptured sundial mounted on a base with steps on each side. The children enjoyed trying to work out the proper time according to the sundial which was legible at that time. It can now be seen just inside the Church main gate where it was fairly recently re-established.

Buchanan Parish Church featured prominently in the lives of most parishioners with family pews, complete with name at the outside end, well filled. Most children attended Sunday School where a sound knowledge of Bible stories was gained. Rev W Lacey was followed later by Rev F H Fulton who, being of an artistic disposition, arranged Nativity plays for the children to perform at Christmas. At a later age we attended a Bible class at the manse, now *Shalloch*, led by Mr Fulton.

Nativity play in the Church.   *Photo: Peter Johnson*

During school holidays and after school hours, when daylight, we children were captivated by the wartime activities taking place around us. Toy tin helmets and wooden toy rifles were the order of the day, and imagining ourselves as real soldiers, we loved to follow the army personnel who were building round shaped corrugated iron storage huts in the surrounding estate woodlands. These were filled with shells and ammunition which were transported by small railway trucks on rails which had been laid in various parts of the woodlands. The children couldn't resist jumping onto these trucks and running them along the rail tracks when the soldiers had gone away. On a more dangerous level temptation led to the taking of cordite from the shells and lighting them like fireworks. When thrown upwards the length of cordite would fly around haphazardly in all directions seemingly following the scattering perpetrators. Eventually the police came to the classroom lecturing us on the danger of such behaviour and strictly forbidding any further involvement. Fortunately, no one had been injured.

Now and again there were children's parades involving slogans for victory. Everyone was attired in fancy dress, creating much interest in the community, especially as there was a prize for the best outfit and slogan.

At several parts of the road between Drymen and Balmaha large concrete, round-shaped barricades were positioned in readiness for any impending invasion. Huge rolls of barbed wire were also there as a possible deterrent to any advancing enemy vehicle but fortunately they were destined not to be used. Several local men were called into the Home Guard and could often be seen practicing for action that thankfully did not materialise. Large searchlights and anti-aircraft guns were a feature of the area, the nearest to Milton being at the field on the Balmaha side of Gartfairn Farm road end. At nights we watched the sky being lit up by these huge beams of light looking for enemy aircraft passing overhead. All buildings and household lights were completely blacked out by law, as were buses and other vehicles. Black blinds had to be drawn at dusk so that enemy aircrew could not use lights on the ground as a guide. No bombs were dropped in the Buchanan area, the nearest being a stray bomb dropped on the Stockiemuir, near to where an anti-aircraft gun was positioned.

Johnny Galbraith, shepherd at *Arrochybeg*, who found the missing Hurricane fighter plane. *Photo: Willie Simpson*

Several British aircraft crashed in the Buchanan area, the most devastating being a Lancaster bomber at the end of the war which after circling around in distress came down hitting the top of the Conich and exploding. The wreckage was scattered over a large area at the back of the Conich and all members of the crew sadly lost their lives. The RAF salvage team were working there for about three months but eventually had to leave the engines which had sunk too deeply into the boggy peat. On another occasion a Hurricane fighter plane, which had been reported missing several weeks before, was found behind the Gualann by John Galbraith, the shepherd at *Arrochybeg*. Again the pilot did not survive. One airman who did luckily survive was the pilot of a Spitfire fighter plane which crash-landed in a field at Gartfairn Farm causing great excitement. The pilot managed to get out safely and leaving the aircraft where it had come to rest, walked down to the farm. We were all having a good look into the cockpit when Willie Ronald, the farmer, appeared saying jokingly that he would not have to plough that field this year referring to the long furrow gouged out by the rotating propeller as it slithered along the ground.

Helping with chores at Milton Farm - tenanted by Mrs Ronald, daughters Marion (Minnie) and Jessie along with their brothers Fulton and Hughie - provided us with much pleasure. Even childish hands were helpful as a great deal of work had to be carried out, especially at harvest time. The cut grass was turned and teased until dry then raked into swathes which were then pulled into piles ready for forking into hayricks. Although horse drawn implements did the bulk of this work, a great deal of it was also accomplished by hand. The ricks were skilfully built on a base of small branches which were scattered around a tripod of sticks tied at the top with twine. These ricks remained in the field until it was time to bring them home to the farm stackyard where they were forked onto a base of branches to form huge haystacks for winter feeding.

Stackyard behind *Mar Achlais*, August 1956.   *Photo: Peter Johnson*

A specially designed flat trolley cart pulled by horse was used to transport the hayricks from the field to the stackyard. After the operator had tipped the trolley up at the front by releasing a lock, the horse, on order, pushed backwards until the tail end of the trolley, now touching the ground, was partly under the rick. Before that, the loose hay around the foot of the rick had to be pulled out so that two wire ropes attached to a rack and pinion at the front of the trolley could be placed around the base and linked together. By operating a lever the hayrick was slowly pulled up the angled trolley base until its weight caused the base to tip back level and lock. While the corn was being cut by a horse drawn binder which cleverly made it into sheaves, tied around the middle with twine, we helped to make stooks which consisted of about six sheaves standing on end placed together in pairs. Later, when completely dry, these sheaves were loaded carefully on to flat wooden carts for transportation to the stackyard where they were beautifully built into round corn stacks. Another big event was when the thrashing mill arrived to thrash the ears from the straw.

During the early years of the war some Italian prisoners of war came from a camp near Gartocharn to work at Milton Farm. They were generally of a cheerful disposition making friends readily with local families. Louis was an expert player of the mandolin, while Joseph although a beautiful singer possessed a rather loud voice. While singing out in the fields a local man commented that he could be heard two miles away. Towards the end of the War, German POWs also came to work on the farm. Fritz, who has revisited Buchanan on several occasions from his present home in Chicago, is best remembered.

Picnic at Ardlui during the War. Left to right: Peter Johnson, Sarah Johnson (mother) holding Marion Johnson, and visiting friends. *Photo: Peter Johnson*

The farm supplied crates of milk for the school, each child receiving a small bottle with a straw at morning break. The homes round about also depended on the farm milk, a member of each family taking a can or a jug to the rear door to be filled each day. As Fulton had a lorry contractor's business he was involved with coal deliveries as well as keeping fuel for all the paraffin, Tilley and Aladdin lamps which were the standard form of lighting before the advent of electricity. Creityhall Farm just up the lane also required our help at times, especially with potato lifting and turnip thinning for which we were paid one shilling per hundred yards in the late 1940s. Bob and Mrs Urquhart were the tenants there and like the Ronald family, brought the most wonderful home baking, such as scones and pancakes, with tea to the workers in the fields. It was so appreciated and enjoyed by all. A large plate of porridge topped with rich creamy milk and eaten around the table in Mrs Ronald's farm kitchen at suppertime made the hard work in the harvest fields well worthwhile.

It is difficult to envisage nowadays but the children used the main road at Milton as a playground for football, rounders, tag, hide and seek and other games. During the week, especially in the evenings, traffic was extremely light but at weekends many more cars, buses, motorbikes and cyclists passed through on the way to Balmaha and Rowardennan. Alexander's Bluebird buses running between Glasgow, Drymen and Balmaha and McKinlay's coaches from Balloch were often packed with passengers on a day's outing. Duplicate buses regularly had to be arranged so that no one was left stranded. Day trip sails on the two paddle steamers *Princess May* and *Prince Edward* were very popular especially as the rail link from Glasgow connected to the pier head at Balloch from where the steamers set sail. Balmaha pier was kept busy being a popular place for joining or leaving the steamer. At Ardlui, a couple of hours could be pleasantly spent having a picnic or walking around before boarding for the return journey. It was possible to disembark at Rowardennan sailing north, climb Ben Lomond and catch the steamer on the return journey. Watching the huge pistons driving the paddles provided much interest for young eyes during the sail.

Netting salmon on Loch Lomond, October 1953. Apart from sea trout and salmon, there is a wide variety of fish, including powan, sometimes called 'land-locked herring'. *Photo: Peter Johnson*

The Boatyard at Balmaha and the nearby Tearoom attracted many afternoon or evening visitors. Hiring a rowing boat or taking a cruise on one of the motorboats proved to be popular pastimes for day-trippers and locals. A wooden footbridge stretching from the jetty across the road from *Balmaha House* to the area of the boat shed allowed pedestrians easy access to the rowing boats and jetties. On Monday and Thursday evenings a salmon net fishing crew comprising of local men led by Mr Alick Macfarlane left the bay on route to the various areas of the Loch where the net had been set and drawn in for many years. The netting was carried out on behalf of Montrose Estates who owned the fishing rights but although salmon or sea trout were netted fairly regularly, some of these expeditions proved to be fruitless. However the wonderful spirit of companionship and humour experienced by the crew more than made up for lack of success or wet nights with fiercely biting midgies.

Net fishing on the Loch. Left to right: Donald Johnson, Jack Gray, John Macfarlane. *Photo: Peter Johnson*

In the winter of 1946-1947 when, due to extremely cold weather, Loch Lomond froze over extensively, the ice in and around Balmaha bay was eleven inches thick. This led to large numbers of people arriving at weekends to skate, play ice hockey and curling, or to simply walk around on the ice. A highlight for many locals was a very skilful demonstration of figure skating given by Fritz the German prisoner of war. His expertise was greatly appreciated by those whose skating ability was somewhat limited to say the least. A similar situation arose during the winter of 1962-1963 when it was possible to walk from the bay to Clairinch and over to Inchcailleach. Unfortunately on one weekend a young man from Glasgow, aged about seventeen years, while skating between the pier and Inchcailleach, dared to go beyond some safety markers which had been placed on the ice. Disappearing through the thinner ice he failed to resurface casting a gloom on an otherwise very special occasion.

To watch the two blacksmiths Tom and Davie Anderson working in the Smiddy at Buchanan Smithy was a fascinating experience. Farmers brought horses from around the whole area to be shod creating a great deal of work for the smiths. The new horseshoes were skilfully forged on the anvil beside a very hot fire which kept the metal red hot while being shaped. When ready they were plunged into cold water to cool, causing a cloud of steam to erupt. The shoe was then nailed onto the horse's hoof which had been prepared by paring it with a sharp knife.

At Milton the Meal Mill was also fully operational, John Campbell being the miller in charge of all machinery involved in this vital service to the community and further afield. Perhaps watching the huge wooden water wheel outside which drove the whole mill when turned by escaping water from the dam at the back was the highlight for the onlooker. Beside the mill stood a large wooden shed which had once been a Sawmill but was now used as a store.

1948 saw the first of many changes at Milton and Buchanan Smithy when ten new council houses were built at each location. Families were happy to be allocated modern homes and quickly settled in the new surroundings. Just after the War, Buchanan Castle was demolished leaving only the walls standing, and some of the military buildings which had been built during the war were converted into homes. Plots of land were sold for private house building, creating a whole new community around the Castle area. In 1958 a further twelve council houses consisting of four, three and two apartments were added at Milton thus changing the original hamlet completely.

New houses built at Buchanan Smithy, 1948. *Photo: James Taggart*

During the 1950s timber merchants James Jones & Sons of Larbert took over the Estate Sawmill at Milton giving employment to a number of local men. Most of the workers, however, hailed from the north and east of Scotland and while here were housed in temporary wooden homes and bothies built beside the Sawmill. These workers were in Buchanan for about ten years which was the time required to cut the mature timber in the area. The incomers integrated successfully some of them joining in village activities such as the Dramatic and Recreation Clubs. Jack Cowie, originally from Huntly, held the foreman's position while his younger brother Dufftin was the finishing sawyer. Allan McIntyre, who was born at Buchanan Smithy but resident now at Milton in one of the new houses, was the slabbing sawyer and had been employed formerly at the sawmill when it was run by the Estate.

When the timber cutting operation ceased much of the vacated woodland was replanted with quick growing soft wood such as spruce and douglas fir. The Forestry Commission, which also planted large areas of forest locally, provided employment for several Buchanan men and women. Some others who had come to work on the planting programme later settled permanently in the district finding other employment.

Meanwhile the Sawmill site at Milton was converted to a successful boat building and repair business by Buchanan-born Angus MacFadyen who had previously worked for many years at Balmaha Boatyard. His brother Duncan built a fine house opposite the boatshed, creating a greatly admired garden from what had been sawdust bings, stacks of timber and wooden huts.

The Amateur Dramatic Club with *Johnny Jouk the Gibbet*. Back row, left to right: Jessie McIntyre, Mgt Anne McLean, Linday Proudfoot, Ian Brown, Bill Pettett; front row, Jim Vickers, Isobel Bradford, D Johnson, Mina Dugdale. *Photo: Peter Johnson*

Several forms of socialising prevailed including the Amateur Dramatic Club with producer Rev F H Fulton. For years following the War an annual public concert, eagerly anticipated by all, was performed on the stage of the Memorial Hall. The various plays, complete with added scenery background constructed by Estate head joiner Tom Ronald and helpers, consisted mainly of one-act Scottish comedies which were a joy to watch. The participating actors, all from Buchanan, provided wonderful entertainment and eventually competed in the Scottish Amateur Dramatic Festivals at various venues. On one occasion they were asked by the late Duke and Duchess of Montrose to perform at Brodick Castle on the Isle of Arran. Musical concerts and Church social gatherings were also held in the Memorial Hall. The late John M Bannerman of *Old Manse*, Balmaha (who became a Liberal peer, Lord Bannerman of Kildonan) was a renowned champion of all things Gaelic He often arranged concerts involving the best-known Gaelic singers of the day. Chairing those events himself, he amused the audience with much wit and charm.

Buchanan SWRI (Scottish Women's Rural Institute) was well supported by the ladies of the community who met together in the hall on Thursday evenings of each month. The Flower Show run by the SWRI and held at the end of August engendered a great deal of interest leading to keen competition in the various classes. Vegetables were widely grown ensuring larger entries in that department but the flower, baking and housewifery classes also excelled. A constant winner was Andrew Donaldson who, with his wife Mary, lived in the *Old Schoolhouse* on the corner. His garden beside the house produced tremendous crops of vegetables and flowers but the highlight was his large greenhouse full of magnificent begonias which won prizes at major flower shows such as Ayr and Stirling. Passing bus tours often stopped to admire the display and to donate to a moneybox situated within the greenhouse for the purpose of helping spastic children. Andrew and Mary certainly had green fingers, but others also produced excellent vegetables and flowers. The 60th Flower Show took place in August 2006.

Buchanan WRI in the 1950s showing, among others, Betty Forbes, Margaret Miller, Mary Ronald, Sarah Johnson, Bessie Stewart, May Perryman.
Photo: Peter Johnson

Buchanan Recreation Club was very popular, being patronized by most of the men within travelling distance. As well as meeting for carpet bowling on the evenings of Wednesday and Saturday in the Memorial Hall, many club members travelled widely to participate in Saturday tournaments which lasted from afternoon until late at night. Buchanan, in common with other surrounding clubs, had its own tournament when rinks from quite far afield would congregate in the hall and schoolroom where the bowling boards were laid out for the competition. Tasty hot pies and tea were provided in the late afternoon but some of the competitors, who were mainly from farming and other rural occupations, would disappear for some time while awaiting their turn for a game. On their return it became obvious that a refreshment or two had been consumed which led to scenes of much humour for the rest of the evening. It must be added that the ability to play skilfully was seldom affected. The Recreation Club is still running today.

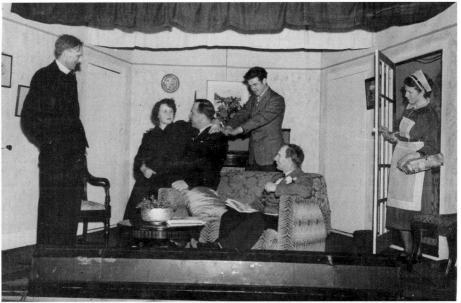

Auld Nick, **29 March 1951. Left to right: Bill Pettett, Betty Bradford, Jimmy Shanks, Donald Galbraith, Isobel Bradford.** *Photo: Peter Johnson*

Bus outings to the Royal Highland Show, which was held at a different venue each year, were very popular. The bus was always filled with people really enjoying the day's outing together. Stopping at a pre-booked hotel for lunch and high tea was greatly appreciated. On the way home singing would break out among the passengers to the accompaniment of a harmonica usually played by Mary Donaldson who had a fine repertoire of well-known songs. Arriving home late at night feeling rather tired, everyone felt satisfied by an enjoyable day spent together.

Radio featured greatly in the lives of the people who listened in intently during the War years. The set required a large dry battery and a wet accumulator which had to be taken to the garage in Drymen once per fortnight for re-charging. Programmes of music and drama as well as news bulletins were very popular but the introduction of television and its eventual spread changed much of life as it had been previously lived. Farming and other rural industries became highly mechanized rendering most of the old methods redundant and vastly reducing the need for manpower.

Amateur Dramatic Club at Kippen Festival, 31 January 1952. Back row, left to right: Betty Bradford, Annie Stewart, Neil Cairns, May Perryman, Jack Cowie, Billy Anderson, Donald Galbraith; front row: Bill Pettett, Mary Watson, Isobel Bradford, D Johnson. *Photo: Peter Johnson*

Full cast of *Auld Nick*, 29 March, 1951. Back row, left to right: Bill Pettett, Neil Cairns, Isobel Bradford, Jimmy Shanks, Betty Bradford, R McLean, Mary Watson, Garry Bradford, Donald Galbraith; front row: D Johnson, May Perryman, Nan Galbraith, Miss Stewart, Liz Rasmussen, Mrs B Ross, Rev F H Fulton (Producer). *Photo: Peter Johnson*

Ronnie Johnson
Buchanan Smithy

Ronnie has lived in Drymen for forty years. His wife is Margaret, daughter of Jack and Margaret Gray of Milton of Buchanan and latterly Balmaha. Eldest son Robert lives in Crieff with wife Elaine and children Blair and Erin. Second son John (Ian) lives in Drymen but presently works in Houston USA. Daughter Anne lives in Callander with husband Garry and daughters Emma, Lana and Isla. Third son David lives and works in Melbourne, Australia. Ronnie worked as a joiner with Montrose Estates, then technical subjects teacher for thirty years at the Vale of Leven Academy.

Photo: Ronnie Johnson

I was born at Buchanan Smithy three quarters of a century ago. My father had died and my mother and my two older brothers Peter and Willie were staying with our maternal grandparents.

Soon after, our family moved from the district but returned when I was five years old to live next door to our grandparents. Our house was the end one, nearest Buchanan.

The Smithy Row consisted of two rows of cottages with the Smiddy itself and a detached house between them, looking much as it is today. Each house at the bottom end consisted of a living room and an upstairs bedroom. We had an extra little room to the rear just big enough to take a double bed. There was a very basic scullery and no running water or sanitation inside, as we know it today. Water was drawn from a standpipe behind the houses. Clothes washing was done in an outhouse which had a coal fired boiler and a hand operated wringer and a mangle. Water was also heated there and brought into the house for the tin bath in which we bathed in front of the kitchen range. There was a communal dry closet behind the houses, which was emptied weekly by an Estate worker. Most families made their own arrangements and had their own private privy down in the

Buchanan Smithy looking east in the 1930s. *Photo: Ronnie Johnson*

The Johnson family 1954. Left to right,
Peter, Ronnie, mother (Jean), Willie.
Photo: Ronnie Johnson

Grandfather William McLean.
Photo Ronnie Johnson

garden. In our case this meant a hundred yard walk in all weathers. The emptying of the privy was often my Saturday job and involved digging a hole in the large garden that went with the property. It's maybe a coincidence, but we grew smashing vegetables. In the summer the water supply often dried up and water had to be fetched in buckets from a nearby spring in the woods. In the winter the supply usually froze up. Winters were always harsher then and summers much drier, or so it seemed.

Behind the row of houses there was a row of byres and a row of pig houses. The only person in the bottom row who kept a cow, in my time, was my grandfather and the pig houses were no longer in use. We did, however, keep hens, which supplied the family with fresh eggs as well as chicken meat. This didn't go down well with me as I had names for them all and I found it hard to have to eat my pets. To this day I find it nearly impossible to eat chicken.

The occupants of the houses were mainly Estate workers or retired Estate workers who paid rent to the Duke of Montrose. Our grandfather had been a gamekeeper with the Estate and had lived at *Coldrach Lodge* before retiral.

The blacksmith Tom Anderson, who lived there with his family, tenanted the house to the west of the Smiddy. He had a double house as he had a very large family.

As children, we played mainly around the doors. The abandoned pig houses were useful for playing various games. The girls had wee hooses in the covered parts and we all played 'tig on the pighooses, last up's het'. The Smiddy ring was used as a dell for playing 'relieve-oh', a game where one person had to catch the rest of the players and place them in the dell. We also played 'kick the can', which was similar to 'relieve-oh'. These games were often played in the dark or moonlight, as streetlights were unheard of. Another favourite was 'hudgie' where one person tried to prevent the rest of the players from crossing the road by bumping them. For this game you had to hop on one leg. We played games of football on the main road, for it was rare to see any traffic on the road. There was no television, wireless was in its infancy and evenings were spent reading, sewing and darning. Yes, even the boys. We also had lots of card games.

The Smiddy itself was a source of great attraction for us, where the shoeing of horses and the repair of farm implements was carried out with great skill. On a wet day especially, there was a queue a horses waiting to be shod and, if you were lucky, you had the job of holding a horse while the farmer was elsewhere. The reward was usually a sixpence. The wooden wheels of the horse-drawn carts had an iron rim or tyre on them, which had to be shrunk, fitted on to the wheel. This was done by making a hoop of steel to the correct diameter, heating it, fitting it to the wheel and then cooling it rapidly to tightly fit the wheel. Men with heavy hammers were needed for that job and this was often accompanied by oaths when the ring didn't fit properly, much to our amusement. The actual fitting was done on the Smiddy ring which was a large circular metal doughnut lying flat on the earth with the earth dug out in the centre. Blacksmith Tom Anderson allowed us on occasion to pump the bellows for the heating of the horseshoes in the forge. At the side of the forge he had a box in which he kept thick black tobacco which he smoked and sometimes chewed. One day, my friend Geordie McNaughton and I thought we would try out the chewing, which also involved spitting. Ten minutes later two very green-faced boys decided that that wasn't for them.

Another favourite play area for us was the forest in front of the Smiddy. The forests had numerous tracks through them that had been made for walks and coaches in the days

Tommy Anderson (left) and Ronnie Johnson, 1940, at the Smiddy. Tommy's father (Tom) was the blacksmith. *Photo: Ronnie Johnson*

Jack Gray (Ronnie Johnson's father-in-law) on the charcoal-fired tractor, mid-1930s.
Photo: Ronnie Johnson

when the Duke occupied *Buchanan Castle*. We made full use of them as cycle runs when we became bicycle owners.

The school for The Smithy children was Buchanan. This involved a daily walk of over a mile each way, quite a feat for five year olds, but there was little choice. There were a lot of distractions for us on the way; bridge walls to be walked, burns and their contents to be explored, resulting in our often-late arrival. There was no avoiding school as Miss Johnston from Drymen came the same way. Even when the road was blocked with snow she collected us on her way past on foot and escorted us to school. There was no such thing as a closed school. Sunday for us meant attending Buchanan Kirk Sunday School and eventually the Kirk itself. I also at one time pumped the bellows for the air driven organ in the Kirk.

On our way home from the school, occasionally we were lucky enough to get a lift on a horse cart and, as cars and vans became more common, a lift in the post van or the baker's van when it was travelling home empty. Secondary schooling was at Balfron, as now, and buses were laid on. It was a matter of pride to get a prize for perfect attendance at school, and it was the only one I ever got.

At Christmas there was a party for the Buchanan children. In my younger days this was held in the Castle. The Duke himself made an appearance and we were shown films, which I recollect were of geographical nature, in black and white. We then were herded in to the kitchens where we all had a good feed. No Santa Claus, but we all got a wee prezzy.

All this changed, of course, when the Second World War broke out. The Castle became a hospital, surrounded by wards. The woods where we had played became one gigantic munitions dump. We still managed to play in the woods secretly and made use of the miniature railway that now occupied our former tracks. When the soldiers went back to barracks we played on a little hand propelled buggy on which we whizzed along the tracks. We could have been blown to bits many times, but survived. Today, no doubt, we would be termed vandals.

One thing that stays very much in my memory is the dreadful nights of the Clydebank blitz when the skyline to the south was ablaze and the noise of the bombs exploding echoed round the hills. In the days that followed, Clydebank families appeared in all modes of transport, uncovered lorries laden with mothers and children, all looking for refuge. Some distant relatives of ours lived with us for a short time before it was safe for them to return home. The school had large influx of pupils and we were put on part time education for a short time.

In time the war ended, but times had changed. The families of The Smithy had grown up. The older generation had died out. The Smithy houses were condemned, and a programme of new housing for The Smithy people was begun. In 1949 the families were moved, and oh what joy to have running hot water, clothes that didn't smell or feel damp. Electricity still hadn't reached The Smithy and there were still the paraffin lamps, but that wasn't a bother.

Over fifty-five years have now passed since my family left The Smithy. We were glad to leave but I am pleased that the old houses have been renovated and brought up to standard and the frontages still remain more or less as they were when we were children.

Duncan McLaren Johnston
Strathcashel

Duncan McLaren Johnston (Mac) is eighty years old and has been married to Margaret for fifty-three years. He has two daughters and four grandchildren.

He apprenticed as an engineer, then went to the Merchant Navy. He returned to work in Burroughs for twenty-five years, then moved on to a job in the Vale of Leven Hospital until he retired.

Duncan's hobbies have included fishing, wrestling, hostelling, rowing, motorbiking and dancing with his wife. He lives in the Vale of Leven.

Photo: Linda Weir

My grandad, Duncan McLaren, his wife Mary and the family, Mary, Dan, Alex, Jean and Malcolm had to leave the island of Eigg around the 1870s, for what reason I do not know. They came to the east side of Loch Lomond and worked for the Duke of Montrose.

My mother, the youngest, was born at *Sallochy Cottage* (now *The Anchorage*) in 1884. *Strathcashel* was built after that and most of the stone used was from the old *Strathcashel House*, about 100 yards to the north of now *Strathcashel*. My grandfather was the first tenant in the present *Strathcashel House*.

My grandmother died about 1890 and is buried on Inchcailleach. My mother's elder sister Mary brought up my mother and my uncle John McLaren.

My mother and uncle John went to school at Sallochy School House at the north end of Sallochy Bay. At that time the Irish tinkers were camped at Sallochy Level. Mother and uncle John would get a great soup from there on the way home from school barefoot. The tinkers were there to strip bark from the wood, the bark then went to the Liquor Works at Balmaha. The wood went down the Loch and Leven to the shipyards, and the twigs, called sprulee, to the iron works to put an anti-rust skin on the steel plates (so I am told).

Duncan McLaren Johnston

My grandad worked for the Duke at the coppicing of oak trees. There were twenty-four plots of oak so they were coppiced every twenty years. Uncle Malcolm also worked planting oak and when he was old enough he became a forester for the Duke. Uncle Dan went to the Loch steamer and became Captain Dan McLaren of the *Princess May*. Uncle Alex worked as a roadman between Balmaha and Rowardennan. Uncle John was a shepherd on the Black Mount and on Rannoch Moor.

My father, James McQueen Johnston, served his apprenticeship with Gray's of Drymen as a saddler. He was saddler to the Duke's horses and racehorses, making pockets for lead weights. He went to France with the army in the First World War as a saddler. When he came home his hearing and eyesight were bad so he had to give up his trade.

We lived in Levenbank Terrace, Jamestown and grandfather, in his old age, came to live with my mother. I was born on 20 January 1927. My grandfather died when I was five years old. He was ninety-five. He is buried on Inchcailleach beside his wife Mary.

Uncle Alex now lived in *Strathcashel* with his sons Duncan (Dochie), Alex, John and daughter Kate. I had been going to *Strathcashel* since I was a toddler, and also every school holiday. My mother would go to milk the cows, look after the family, make the butter etc. to give Kate a wee holiday. I loved it.

Strathcashel, 2007   *Photo: James Taggart*

Uncle Alex was my hero, I thought he could do everything and his stories were marvellous. Uncle Dan told good tales about Eigg, but uncle Alex was enthralling.

We would go out for the cow at 6pm for milking. She could be anywhere on the hillside but by wind and weather he knew where she would be. The cow would not come for me. "See", he would say, "you have the smell of the Vale, all their dye works." On the way back over the hill from *Critreoch* he would show me Fairy Rocks, and at *Strathcashel*, the Fairy Ring where the Queen gives her orders to the working fairies and where they hold their parties and dances. He got angry if I said, "I don't believe it." "Oh, they're here alright, you had better believe it if you live here." He was a great man.

Cashel farm with *Strathcashel* on the Loch shore.   *Photo: Willie Simpson*

One day two walkers came over the hill from *Critreoch*; the dog alerted us to strangers. Uncle Alex went out to see who it was and they produced a bottle of whisky and offered Alex a drink. He took the bottle and started to tell them how lucky they were to get past the witch of *Critreoch* and about the little people on the hill. After the tale (just long enough for him to finish the whisky) he handed them back the empty bottle and said they had better be on their way before dark. We watched them go past the old house that he told them had been haunted. I enjoyed the story with the visitors but after they were gone he said, "daft folk; believe that, they'll believe anything".

At night after we had eaten, with the oil lamp carefully lit (no one touched the lamp except Alex, as it had very fine glass), if it was a dark night, no moon and still, no wind, he would sit quiet and smoke his pipe by the wood fire. I would sit on the fender at his side, listening to his stories. When he had finished his smoke of thick black tobacco he would give me a kick to say, "come on then". I'd pick up my wee sack and follow him out and walk behind him. No noise No talk. I'd have no idea where we were going; maybe a burn where he had seen a fish or a tree where a pheasant roosted. One night he finished his pipe and out we went. We sat on a dyke behind the old house. We sat there for ages till he tapped me on the shoulder. No talk. I followed him, but we went back home. I was full of questions but couldn't ask till we sat down at the fire. When I did ask, he gave me that look and I knew what he was thinking – a silly wee Vale boy that smelled of the dye-house. "Did you no smell the smoke?" he said. "No", I replied. He just shook his head. There was somebody about, they had been smoking, so we just came home. We were going (I heard later) to 'smeek' a pheasant out a tree.

I asked him about the witch at *Critreoch*, as only my cousin Malcolm McLaren and big Jean lived there, and Jean - who was always ill - never got out of bed in the outhouse. Back in my mother's time at *Strathcashel*, the woman that lived there was called the 'Spey Wife'. She worked with herbs and wild plants; people would go to her for something for a cough or whatever. She was known for a vendetta with adders. If you had seen a snake, not just adders (the only poisonous snake in Scotland) she would go early and wait for it coming out in the morning to sun itself to get started. She had a hazel stick with a forked end (like a 'Y'). She would catch the snake and kill it. What she did with it then I don't know, and neither did my mother. That's where the witch of *Critreoch* came from.

Critreoch, 2007. No witches now? *Photo: James Taggart*

When I was thirteen, uncle John came to live with us at Jamestown. He had throat cancer and was attending the Western Infirmary for radiation treatment, but it was terminal. It was a sad time waiting for him to die and his biggest worry was his four dogs. He had three good working dogs. He wrote to other shepherds and they were pleased to take them. The other dog was too old. He just guarded the Bothy and lay at the back door to keep the draught out. I never did hear what happened to him, probably shot, as he would only obey uncle John. My uncle died when I was thirteen years old and is buried in the Vale cemetery.

Uncle Alex died when I was fourteen, that would be 1941. The funeral to Inchcailleach is another story. I'll never forget it. I've been to plenty of burials in my time. I even did bodies up for burials at sea. But I'll never forget uncle Alex's on Inchcailleach on a foggy winter's day.

Mary Hope is my cousin (aunt Jean's daughter). Aunt Jean married a Glasgow policeman and lived in Glasgow. They had a family of four, Duncan, Mary, John and Bunty (Walker). Mrs Mary Hope had a car and took my father and me to *Strathcashel*. Uncle Alex was in his coffin in the house. The minister said a few words, then the men had a dram. The coffin was taken down the large field to a Macfarlane motorboat at the rock. The women stayed in the house to make dinner. The coffin was on two oars across the gunnels of the boat. We sat round it, our knees under the coffin. The day suited the mood of the moment; it was flat calm, the mist right down to the Loch. If you went too far out you lost sight of land, so we went along the shore to Balmaha. No one spoke or smoked, just sat, then across to Inchcailleach. There was no jetty then. The boat men got the coffin off the boat, put the two oars and ropes under the coffin, to be carried by four men, two each side.

We started up the steep path; it was just a single path at that time, so the coffin bearers walked in the bracken on each side of the path. My father had a bad heart, so I took his place. We were half way up at a very steep part when uncle Alex slid down inside his coffin; I still remember the sound. The two at the back, my cousin Eric Billet and me, had all the weight. At the top of the path is a horseshoe bend back to the graveyard where the bearers changed. I'm told at one time this was the place to stop for another dram of locally made whisky.

The McLaren graves are just at the left hand side as you go in the gate although most of the gravestones have now been removed. Uncle Alex's grave had been dug by a rather strange looking man, a big man, high on one shoulder. The soil from the grave had very large stones or rocks; it must have been hard to dig. The coffin was laid in the grave and the Minister said a few words. We were all wet, feet and legs soaked with walking off the path. We left the graveyard to get back to the boat at the Balmaha end of the island. By path, you go south to the horseshoe bend, then down the steep path. As you go down the path it passes quite close to the graveyard above you. I remember it was a very still misty day. We could hear the noise of breaking wood. It must have been the gravedigger filling in the grave with the big stones. I have a mental picture of uncle Alex holding a big stone in his lap. The sail seemed a very long way back.

Back at the house the women had the dinner ready. The men were having a well-deserved dram. My father, who was teetotal, looked over at me. I must have been a wreck. He came over and held out his whisky. I took it, unsure, as everyone was looking at me. So I swallowed it 'like a man'. And coughed and coughed. It got a good laugh, but not from me.

Kirk service on Inchcailleach among the old gravestones, to mark the Millennium.
Photo: Willie Simpson

Ruth MacKenzie, Duchess of Montrose, Chrissie Bannerman and Sheena McAllister at the Millennium service on Inchcailleach. *Photo: Willie Simpson*

Rena Kerr
Buchanan Smithy

Rena Kerr is 98 years old and lives in Buchanan Smithy. Born in Croftamie, for many years she was a hairdresser in Glasgow. Her brother Tom Kerr owned the Rowardennan Hotel and set up the first-ever garage in Drymen.

Photo: Laurie Lilburn

I was born in Croftamie on 12th July 1909. My father was a stonemason and I had two brothers, Jimmy who was twelve years older and Tommy who was ten. I attended the primary school at Croftamie but I have no recollection of this other than playing rounders after school. I did not like this as much as I enjoyed reading and I used to sit at our front window reading and watching rounders in progress in the road outside.

My best friend was Nell Buchanan who later became Nell Aitken, whose husband owned the Wayfarers in Croftamie, and whose children were Buchanan and Noreen. Nell's parents must have been fairly well off because they had a maid who lived in one of the cottages near the River Endrick. I used to stay at Nell's house most evenings where I had supper and we had a rare old time jumping around in her bedroom.

When the 1914/18 War came, my brother Jimmy went into the army and went to France, where he lost a leg. I have very little recollection of this period but later I went to school in the Vale of Leven. We all travelled by steam locomotive to Balloch but the train stopped at Caldarvan Station near Gartocharn where we picked up more local children. Once we got to Balloch we had to cross a bridge to pick up the Glasgow train, which took us to the Vale of Leven. My only recollection of school days is that my full name took up more space than there was on my examination papers and this was always causing a problem. One day a boy called Archie Mackie was sent by the Headmaster to get a girl called Cathy Kerr and this caused much tittering in class because to us there was no such person. I was then, and still am, Rena Kerr.

After leaving school, I went off to the top floor of the Albany Buildings near Charing Cross in Glasgow where I was taught hairdressing which was to be my job for most of my life.

About this time there were regular Balls in the *Castle* at Buchanan to which my mother and father were invited, as were all the local trades people for whom they were held. Although I visited the *Castle*, I was never invited to one of the Balls. I remember about then that the Loch froze over and it was possible to walk out to Inchcailleach.

Meantime, my brother Tommy married Christine and they had a son whom they called Jimmy. Tommy opened the garage in Drymen, which had petrol pumps, and he hired a van-like vehicle with which he picked up and delivered people to the railway station at Croftamie. One of his customers was Edward Collins the paper maker from Kelvindale in Glasgow, who at that time owned the shooting lodge at Rowardennan which is now the Youth Hostel. I am told that when the whole family arrived their luggage came by cart. There was a permanent staff at the Lodge. At that time, the Collins family owned the Hotel too, but it was run by a Glasgow firm which started life as temperance group who bought the very worst of Glasgow's public houses, cleaned them up, and refurbished them.

Tommy meantime had branched out and bought *Balmaha House* and the large timber-built tearoom there, which was right on the Lochside (now a picnic area taken over by the Local Authority). The Tearoom had living accommodation for the several waitresses who worked there and who served in the shop next door. Tommy put in petrol pumps and the maid in *Balmaha House* was expected also to attend to the pumps which did not please her! Some time later Tommy bought the Rowardennan Hotel from Edward Collins and he and his family went to live there. The Hotel had a shop and a post office, operated the school bus and the ferry to Inverbeg. Many's the wild night I had at Rowardennan where all the local folk met for a good dram and a good crack. The bar had to close early in those days but we all just moved through to the kitchen!

I suppose now I will have to give you my full name: Catherine Donaldina Margaret McInnes Kerr.

Rowardennan Hotel, 2007.   *Photo: James Taggart*

Laurie Lilburn
Sallochy

Laurie Lilburn was born in Glasgow in 1928, and moved to east Loch Lomond in 1970. A valuer to trade, he also ran the Rowardennan Hotel for three years. He lived at the Old School *at Sallochy, now* Sallochy House, *for thirty years before passing it on to his helicopter pilot son, Kevin. He has been deeply immersed in community affairs for all of that time.*

Photo: Jenny Taggart

I first went to Rowardennan, by road, in 1970. Before that my experience of Loch Lomond had always been by boat as most of my weekends had been spent on Inchmurrin. I went to Rowardennan to assist a friend to buy the Hotel and used my connections to have valuations and other enquiries to be made, only to find that my 'friend' did not have the necessary funds. I was out of pocket and, by this time, had fallen in love with the east side of Loch Lomond. Fortunately, my wife Wilma and son Kevin (aged 4) shared my enthusiasm. I brought together a small consortium of like-minded friends and bought the Hotel.

In our time the Hotel was successful and, in particular, our folk singer Steve Middell, packed the Big Bar every Thursday and Sunday evenings, summer and winter. Through the winter rooms were let, sometimes, for as little as £1 a night. Better for the bar trade and safer for the road! At that time the Hotel ran the school bus, for which I failed my test to get a PSV licence, and we also had the right to operate a 'Queen's Ferry' between Rowardennan and Inverbeg. The ferry was an old converted, wartime steel lifeboat until one afternoon in summer, vandals went aboard and set it on fire. Unfortunately, it drifted under the pier in which a large hole was burned. Our other much-treasured right was to draw a net for salmon and sea trout for the Hotel table, and I have fond memories of taking my turn at the leads or in the boat setting the net while being eaten alive by midgies.

It was clear to us that Rowardennan was worthy of greater things and we employed architects and environmentalists to enable us to redevelops the whole area. Three years of going round in circles with planners who had no idea what they wanted done and only knew how to say "no" was enough for me and I sold out. However, by then my family and I knew that we had to stay, and in 1973 I bought the *Old School* at Sallochy, which I modernised and made it our home. At that time, the only water supply was from our own burns but thanks to the untiring efforts of Mrs McLaren of Critreoch, the Water Board was forced, I think by the Secretary of State, to run a pipe from Balmaha to Rowardennan. Meantime, the North of Scotland Hydro Electric Board was planning a 1600 megawatt pumped storage hydro scheme for the west side of Ben Lomond in an area known as Craigroystan. From my own knowledge of a similar scheme at Loch Awe, I knew that, from an engineering point of view, this was an excellent plan, given that much of our electricity then would be from atomic stations and a pumped storage scheme was just what was needed to meet periods of peak demand. However, during the consultation process it became clear that the disruption on the whole of the east side of the Loch would be enormous and that work would be likely to last for around twenty years. I calculated that, if a Lochside road was used, a heavy vehicle for men and materials would pass my roadside house every one and a half minutes, twenty four hours every day. I was definitely not in favour of this. There were suggestions to build an entirely new road higher up away from the Loch, using the rail terminal at Balloch and a ferry service from there, or the use of the main road on the west side, which was badly in need of upgrading, and then using ferries for the short journey across near the head of the Loch. Nothing was ever decided. There was a fall in the demand for electricity and the whole project was shelved in 1980.

Sallochy House, once the Old School.   *Photo: Laurie Lilburn*

The 'Friends of Loch Lomond' was founded by Mrs Donald Colquhoun and Mrs Hannah Stirling in 1978 to object, in the strongest possible terms, to the building of this power station. They gained worldwide support and their Chair, Mrs Hannah Stirling was reported to be delighted by the decision by North of Scotland Hydro Board not to proceed. Among the declared objects of the Group was 'to cherish, protect and enhance the natural beauty, amenity and character of Loch Lomond, its islands and surrounding countryside.' They have never wavered from this objective and have gone on from strength to strength giving support where they thought it was deserved, criticism when they thought it appropriate and promoting initiatives such as an archaeological survey of the islands, new walks etc. Occasionally, they themselves attract criticism for being too negative in their approach to change but a balance has to have two sides.

The now world famous West Highland Way, a footpath stretching for around 100 miles between Milngavie, just north of Glasgow, and Fort William, was opened in 1980 and this has proved to be a great success. An estimated 100,000 people complete the journey each year providing a year-round source of income for hotels and bed and breakfast establishments on the way.

Red deer on the West Highland Way at Rowardennan.   *Photo: Internet*

Not everyone realises that long before the road on the west side of Loch Lomond became the established route between north and south, the way to go was the path along the east side of the Loch. Drovers bringing their cattle to market at Stirling from the north would come down the west side as far as Inverbeg, and, using a lead animal tied to a rowing boat, would swim their herds across to Rowardennan. It is said that Rob Roy and his brothers often frequented the Inn there.

In 1981 the Loch Lomond Association was founded by Jack Bisset (of Inverbeg Hotel) and I, and many other interested parties became members. This was in response to a fear that the proposed new Regional Park Authority would seek to pass byelaws, some of which could be to zone or impose speed limits. The Association prepared, and had distributed, a Code of Conduct which, it was hoped, would stave off these and other restrictive measures. As time went by this was revised and proved to be a valuable guide as to the use of the Loch by boat owners.

An interesting event in 1981 was the discovery at Sallochy of two raccoons which were at first thought to be badgers. However, despite all round disbelief, they were proved to be raccoons and eventually they were found to have walked all the way round from Cameron House where they were the personal pets of Patrick Telfer Smollett whose men spent many days and nights trying to trap them. They were very friendly, almost lovable, little creatures and thoroughly enjoyed living on dog food for about two months. Eventually, my son Kevin and I trapped them using an old badminton net. Tears were shed when they were taken back to Cameron House.

I was active in the Buchanan Community Council and took over from the Duke of Montrose as chairman. In those days community councils did not have the same powers or obligations as they do now but we were concerned with all things affecting our parish. We were a pressure group for something to be done about Milarrochy Bay that had become a haven for undesirables and greatly overcrowded on good weekends, both on the land and in the water. I was asked to take a party of MPs to see things for themselves and on the day concerned there were swimmers, sail boards, jet bikes and speedboats all sharing the same water. It took seven years to get the facilities and control there is now.

East Lochside on a busy summer day.   *Photo: Willie Simpson*

In July 1986, Malcolm Rifkind, the then Secretary of State for Scotland, announced the formation of the Loch Lomond Regional Park and one of the many matters which received prominence on their agenda was byelaws for Loch Lomond. In June 1992 they set up a Byelaw Advisory Group of which I was a member and a technical adviser to the Park Authority. The byelaws produced were well received and would have worked well had the laws relating to inshore speed limits ever been enforced. The misgivings of the Loch Lomond Association proved to be well founded, as was highlighted by the debacle of the National Park's proposals for the revision of the byelaws in 2005. This led to the formation of a new organisation called FAIRPLAY calling for the enforcement of the existing byelaws before any attempt should be made to introduce new, seriously restrictive and unnecessary laws which may not be enforced any more rigorously than the previous ones. To date no one has ever been convicted of breaking a speed limit.

Early in the 1990s I obtained the agreement of every landowner between Balmaha and Rowardennan not to allow the launching of jet bikes from their land. The only one who would not agree was the Regional Park, who, by that time controlled Milarrochy Bay. Who is sorry now?

In April 1994, I invited the known landowners around the Loch to a meeting from which it was agreed to set up an organisation open only to those who owned parts of the foreshore of the Loch, the banks of its tributaries or the islands. It was decided to call the association The Riparian Owners of Loch Lomond (TROLLS) and its primary purpose was to protect the interests of its members.

1994 turned out to be a very bad year. My wife Wilma, to whom I had been married for thirty-eight years, died after a long struggle against cancer. She was a very brave lady and supported me in all my undertakings connected with the Loch. She was well known for our days at the Hotel and the many local events such as the Drymen Show, and she was greatly missed.

Wilma Lilburn, 1984.
Photo: Laurie Lilburn

In terms of the Civic Government (Scotland) Act 1982, any Local Authority seeking to impose byelaws on any inland waterway (which included Loch Lomond) required to have the approval of everyone who had a proprietorial interest. During the summer of

1994, TROLLS became aware of the fact that a late addition to the Local Government (Scotland) Bill, then before Parliament (in Westminster) would, without any form of consultation or prior notice, remove this right of veto. Attempts were made to have an amendment made, but by misrepresentation and political chicanery, the amendment proposed was withdrawn and the Bill passed before TROLLS knew. At that time there was only one maintained objection to the byelaws proposed.

In March 1997, TROLLS set up the Erosion Study Group (which involved numerous outside agencies) to study the causes of Lochside erosion and, if possible, to seek ways of combating it. We studied weather records as far back as the mid 1800s, Loch level and rainfall records, the original Water Order giving the Water Board the right to extract water and other relevant data. It is difficult to convey the amount of time spent by a few dedicated people to gather masses of information from which it was possible to make informed assumptions as to the cause of the problem and what might be done about it.

Laurie Lilburn at home with his dog Indie (she was born on 4 July).   *Photo: Laurie Lilburn*

Our first important discovery was that in the twenty-five years before 1995 (i.e. twenty-five years after the barrage on the Leven) the average winter rainfall had increased by 25 percent and was increasing. This was not something which could have been foreseen by the engineers who planned the barrage construction. Even then, it seemed that the record Loch level of 33'3" reached in March 1990 was probably a one-off. It was revealed that the most serious erosion occurred when there were high Loch levels combined with high winds. The myth that erosion was being caused by waves from passing boats was dispelled once and for all. The way in which the barrage was being operated contributed to the creation of higher Loch levels than would have occurred had it been operated in a different way, a view which was not then accepted by the Water Board or SEPA. A fund was opened to enable TROLLS to employ a hydrologist capable of utilizing the computerised model of the Loch held by the Water Board and after £3,000 was raised, SNH agreed to match this amount and cover any additional funding required. While these negotiations were under way, the Water Board announced that they were working on a new model and when this was available they, themselves, ran the programmes TROLLS had requested, which proved that their contentions were correct.

As a result of joint discussions with the Water Board and SEPA, new ways of operating the barrage were developed which allowed for a build up of water supplies when they will be most needed with a gradual run down of the amount stored in the Loch to the lowest practical level prior to the onset of the winter rainfall. Until December 2006 this appeared to be working well and TROLLS started on their remaining objective, which was to have the operation of the barrage automated.

November 2006 proved to be the wettest month in Britain since records began (here 316 mm.) but in December the new record here became 421 mm. The Loch rose to the highest level ever recorded, 33'5.2" (10.22 metres) with resultant widespread damage and serious disruption to businesses. What the level would have been had the barrage not been completely down from September is a matter for conjecture.

The Erosion Study Group commenced further studies in January 2007, but it is now too early to predict whether or not we will find an answer to the possible effects of global warming on future rainfall in the Loch Lomond catchment area and the high Loch levels which are to be anticipated.

I have chosen not to include my recollections of the days, weeks and years spent on assisting with the development of the Loch Lomond Regional Park, the Steering Committee for the subsequent Loch Lomond and the Trossachs National Park and the recent activities of the new National Park Authority. Some of their initiatives to promote tourism, deal with the increasing litter problem, and a serious problem with vandalism caused primarily by overnight visitors in cars, have already had some success but still have a long way to go. On the other hand, their ill informed and misguided attempts to appear to be dealing with problems on the Loch have met with stiff opposition and it remains to be seen if they will accept the guidance which has been offered.

Angus MacFadyen
Milton of Buchanan

Angus MacFadyen was born in Buchanan parish and has lived and worked there all his life. He owns and operates the Boatyard at Milton of Buchanan. He has been a mainstay of the community for many years, and was recognised by the Provost's award for community service in 2006.

Photo: Jenny Taggart

I was born at *High Auchmar* on 28 February 1928. When I was six months old my parents moved down to Milton to one of the four houses that were the only ones there at that time, apart from the *Milton Farmhouse* and the *Old Schoolhouse*.

Our neighbours were the Ronald family in their farm, Mr And Mrs John Campbell in the next end house, then next was Mr John Mitchell, then ourselves and Mrs Findlay and her son Gilbert. One of my first memories was of Johnnie Mitchell taking photographs of a family group with a camera on a tripod and plates and a flash. I was curious why he had to go under a hood when he took the photographs. Shortly after he was drowned in the Mar Burn when he fell into the burn, which was in spate. He had come off the bus at night and mistaken the light of the *Old Schoolhouse* for The Milton. As the bus had taken him past the farm road he had gone in the second entrance to the Meal Mill and over the bank. Fulton Ronald found him next day lodged in the stepping-stones down The Mains field.

Donald Johnson and his new wife Sarah then moved into that house and were our neighbours for years.

I started school early at three and a half or four years old as I used to follow Juliet Campbell to school. So, Mr Ballantyne the headmaster told my mother, "Just let him come along and he can sit in with the primary classes." Miss Spittal was the primary teacher. Miss J Macfarlane was assistant teacher.

The school was what was called a Higher Grade School. The Lower Grade Secondary School is now the general purposes room in the present school. The Primary School was in the house now called *Burnside Cottage*. The senior pupils quite often got lessons in the Museum and Library, now the Memorial Hall.

The Library, now the small hall, had glass cases of stuffed birds, butterflies, insects, grasses, coins, and a large case of stuffed animals in the centre: fox, badger, otter, stoat, weasel, hare, rabbit, roe deer etc. Along the left wall, looking from the door, and on the wall next to the school were shelves of books, which pupils could use in their studies. On a good day you went up an outside staircase on to the flat roof to study in the open air. The roof was surrounded by a parapet with small diamond shaped openings to look through, like a fort or castle.

The Museum entrance hall had a stand with various guns from different ages and the main hall had cases of exhibits from scenes of Indian villages to artefacts from many different countries including a velocipede cycle, which we would try to ride around the balcony.

One memory was of going to a sports day at Drymen on the Silver Jubilee of King George V and Queen Mary. We ran races and afterwards went to the Forresters Hall, now the Spar shop, where we all got a large mug with the King, Queen and 'Silver Jubilee 1935' on it and a goodie bag.

Another memory was going up the Lochside to Lochan Maoil Dhuinne to watch Kaye Don attempt to break the world water speed record. I don't think he managed it, not that day anyway. Sir Malcolm Campbell tried also but failed. They could not get calm enough water.

In 1936-37 I contracted TB in my left leg and was taken to Bannockburn Hospital where I spent the next three years until war broke out and I was evacuated home.

The lighting in the school up to 1936 was by gas. There was a small corrugated iron shed (the gas shed) at the back of the school on the bank of the burn and the gas was manufactured by carbide. When I got back to school in the 1940s the lighting was by pressure lamps.

Buchanan Castle was turned into a military hospital. The churchyard was enlarged to make room for a military yard section, now part of the graveyard. The Army took over Balmaha Tearoom for billets for the soldiers who manned the searchlight battery at Braeval. The Tearoom stood where the picnic area is now. There was a lookout position at the top of Craigie Fort. Then the whole district became an ammunition dump with small corrugated iron shelters holding cordite and shells. There were also small railway lines through some of the woods at Buchanan Smithy and below High Mains to the suspension bridge. These were two-foot gauge lines.

There were several aircraft crashes in the district. A Spitfire crash-landed at Gartfairn, a Hurricane at the shoulder of The Guallan, a Fairy Battle on Inchcailleach, a Lockheed Hudson on Bein Uird and an Avro Lancaster on Conich Hill. The Spitfire pilot and the Fairy Battle pilot escaped with little injury.

Patrol boats were based on the Loch to defend against air invasion and Catalina flying boats sometimes landed.

Angus MacFadyen

In 1934-35 Buchanan School became a primary school only and secondary pupils went to Balfron. When I left school in 1946 I started work with Mr. Alick Macfarlane. I was taught to repair wooden boats by his father John Macfarlane who in earlier days had taught woodworking at Buchanan School. I was trained in boat handling and mechanics by Alick Macfarlane. I worked there for nineteen years, taking pleasure trips around the Islands, sometimes doing the Mail Boat if Alick was on holiday. We often carried various cargoes to the Islands and around the Loch on the old cattle boat, like a very large broad rowing boat. Cargoes could vary from cattle, sheep, pigs, feeding stuffs, hay, straw, wool bags from *Cailness* up by Inversnaid, cable laying for the Telephone Company and flittings to the Islands and *Cailness* and *Rowchoish*. Cargoes also included tractors and caravans to Inchfad and a Caterpillar tractor across the Loch at Tarbet to *Rowchoish*.

Alick Macfarlane, 1970. *Photo: Willie Simpson*

When I left Macfarlane's in 1964 I started my own boat repair yard in the Sawmill Yard at Milton of Buchanan.

During the time I worked at Balamha there were three or four islands occupied most of the time. The largest, Inchmurrin, was owned by the Scott family. Inchfad had four owners in that time. Inchcruin was owned by Malcolm Irvine who spent the last four years of his life there. Inchtavannach, Inchconnachan and Inchlonaig were owned by the Colquhoun Estates. Ann Davison, who lived with her husband on Inchfad for three or four years, wrote a book based on her stay there called *Home was an Island*, and another called *Last Voyage* after her husband was drowned in the English Channel and she was lucky to survive.

Angus MacFadyen

Angus MacFadyen at work in his Boatyard, 1972.   *Photo: Willie Simpson*

The year 1946-47 saw a very bad winter. The Loch froze over in early February and was frozen for a month. The ice in the bay at Balmaha was 9-10 inches thick and there were a lot of skaters and curlers enjoying the ice. We had to cut the *Lady Jean* out of the ice all the way to the pier where there was open water in order to go to Bandry Bay to help launch a 56 ton tug which was brought up by road from the Thames to tow barges with sand and gravel from Drumkinnon Bay at Balloch; that was on 9 March 1947.

Going back to The Milton, when I came home from hospital another house had been built, *Mar Achlais*, and the Johnsons had moved in there. Mr and Mrs Jock Gray had moved into the one they had left. The Sawmill had moved across the road from the Meal Mill and was driven by a steam engine instead the water wheel. It later burned down and was rebuilt using electric power when the Hydro Power came to the district. The Church had also been rebuilt after being destroyed by fire in 1938. Sparks from the boiler house had ignited leaves in the gutters, as it had been a very dry summer. The firemen could not get enough water from the burn as it was so low.

During the dry weather in the summer the water supply which came from a tank at Creityhall Farm would go dry and we carried water from a spring at the side of the burn opposite the house *Dunleen*. It never went dry and was very good water.

At the start of the war we were issued with gas masks and Identity Cards; this was the start of National Insurance numbers. Children were evacuated from the town. Some were placed with local families, others were billeted at *Montrose House* for some time. Then most of them went back home to the town.

The Headmistress at the school when I went to hospital was Mrs Black, who had succeeded Mr Ballantyne, and her assistant teacher was Miss Bishop who later married Dr Maud McKinnon's locum (Dr Donald) and left the district. Miss J Johnson replaced her for quite a number of years.

Fire at Buchanan Church, 1938. *Photo: Willie Simpson*

Buchanan Church today. *Photo: Willie Simpson*

In 1950 ten new houses were built at The Milton and several young local couples who had come back from the services and married along with other locals were allocated these houses. The same number were built at Buchanan Smithy so the young men and women coming back from the services had a home in their own district.

In 1948-49 Mr Malcolm Irvine asked the Post Office if a mail service could be provided to the Islands on the Loch as there were three or four islands occupied at that time, and so the Mail Boat started to deliver mail two days a week. Mr Alick Macfarlane ran the boat summer and winter and rarely missed a delivery. Later on in 1950s and 60s another thirteen houses were built at The Milton, so from four cottages it has become a small village.

The *Marion* on the postal run to the Islands.   *Photo: Willie Simpson*

Alick Macfarlane delivers the mail on Inchmurrin, 1973.   *Photo: Willie Simpson*

A younger (and dafter!) Angus MacFadyen does motorbike tricks with Keith Meara, Alan Ferrie, Barry Macfarlane and Heather Watson. *Photos: Angus MacFadyen*

John Macfarlane
Balmaha

John Macfarlane was born in 1936 in Balmaha. He is a Doctor of Physics and worked in Australia for many years as a research scientist. He has been married to Christine since 1963. Christine, children Linda, Kirsti and Gregor, grandchildren Bethany, Tegan, Lachlan and Callum all live in Australia. John is a Senior Research Fellow at Strathclyde University and the National Physical Laboratory. He lives part of the year in Australia and part at his home in Balmaha.

Photo: John Macfarlane

In 1936, I came into a world which was steeped in remnants of past times, the country just recovering from the Depression, and I imagine my parents were already becoming aware of the gathering storm clouds over Europe. But for a few years at least, my earliest memories were of warm days and swallows circling in summer skies.

My grandfather John (right in the photo, with his brother Willie, about 1900: photo courtesy of John Macfarlane), who was skipper of the Duke's steam yacht *Violet* for many years, was approaching his 80th birthday when I first became aware of him. He had stayed with boats and boating long after the yacht was consigned to the breaker's yard after the First World War, and built up the boat-hiring business that has thrived to the present day. John was one of five children born and raised in *The Point* cottage, which still stands just above the present Boatyard. He had attended Buchanan School, and in his youth, served before the mast in ocean-going square-rigged ships crossing the Atlantic.

Back home in the 1890s, he had married and settled

124

down in *Violet Cottage*, which was one of several cottages provided for workers on the Estate. His elder brother James worked as the electrician at Buchanan Castle in the 1920s, where one of the earliest generators in the country was driven by a water-turbine. James built his cottage, *Loch Sloy*, where I now live, next-door to *Violet Cottage*, in 1927. The eldest brother William was the pier-master at Balmaha Pier which in the early 1900s provided the main means of transport from Balmaha. Two or more paddle steamers ran all year round, and connected with the railway at Balloch. The journey to Glasgow was somewhat faster than it is by public transport at the present day.

My father Alexander (Alick) was born in *Violet Cottage* in 1907, and attended Buchanan School which at that time, provided higher education up to year 6, qualifying him (and his older sister Jessie) to go on to University. He evidently chafed at the academic life, however, and around 1930 returned to join his father in the now-expanding boat-hiring business in Balmaha Bay.

My mother, Margaret (Maggie) Barbour, was born in Gartfairn in 1912, into a farming family. She had an older brother John, a younger brother Archie, and three younger sisters Minnie, Elsie and Cissie. When she was about fourteen years old, her mother died, and she left school to help with the housework and chores around the farm.

Boats, gales, snows, frost, fishing, swimming in sun-steeped summer waters, day trips up the Loch on the paddle-steamers, - Loch Lomond, its shores and islands, hills and glens, birds and fishes, indelibly woven into my earliest memories. My brother Barry, just a few years younger than me, was a constant sparring-partner and playmate in a life that seemed full of optimism for the future until the war years cast a huge, ominous cloud over everything.

Alick Macfarlane in Kelvin launch *Duchess of York*, Balmaha Bay, 1930.
Photo: John Macfarlane

John Macfarlane

For about five or six years, all food was rationed. My mother had to register with a particular shop for the basic necessities, such as eggs, sugar, bread, meat, fruit and vegetables. I remember it was Drymen Post Office, run by Mr and Mrs Douglas for the groceries. There was Gowans the baker, and Duncan McEwan the butcher. I also remember Miss Liddell and Miss Bilsland had smaller grocery shops too. Fortunately, my mother's family (who had moved from Gartfairn to Kintyre in the 1930s) had a farm there, *Machribeg*, and we used to get extra supplies of potatoes. My mother kept hens, so we had supplies of eggs and the occasional roast chicken for a treat. My father, too, did the salmon netting for the Estate on the Loch, and salmon (in summer) was often served for dinner. When salmon were scarce, there were usually ample quantities of powan - delicious, small white fish - but they had to be cooked straight away. Sadly, powan are now an endangered species due to the careless introduction of rudd and other foreign fish to the Loch in the 1970s. Fuel for the hearth was rationed too, but there were always fallen trees in the woods, and driftwood on the islands, to stoke up the fires in the cold winter months.

Balmaha Bay, May 1984.   *Photo: Willie Simpson*

Glasgow and Clydebank, of course, were prime targets for the Luftwaffe, and I have vivid memories of hiding under the bed-clothes as the planes droned overhead, often followed by heavy explosions as the bombs found their targets. Even more scary, when the raid was over, the planes, running for home, would drop their surplus bombs at random. Some fell in the Loch, and others blasted two craters in the Stockiemuir Road, just above the *Dualt* cottage, which were never completely filled in for years. At least one plane came down behind the Conich. I remember my father, who was an air-raid warden, bringing home a piece of twisted metal from it. I can't remember if it was German or British, however.

Captain Alick Macfarlane and his dog   *Photo: John Macfarlane*

A small fleet of patrol boats, possibly commandeered from their pre-war owners, was based in Balmaha Bay, and my father had the task of ensuring they were sea-worthy. I can remember a few picnic trips that developed while test-running their engines. As children at school, we became accustomed to seeing convoys of Army trucks going up and down the road. Munitions dumps (corrugated iron structures like Nissen huts) appeared in many secluded woodlands and fields. Some of the more daring boys would raid them during lunch break, and bring back sticks of cordite to set off explosions behind the Playshed. No wonder the teachers were driven almost to distraction at times.

In January 1941 I was five, and started school later the same year. I don't recall being aware that school existed, until my first day there. I remember being directed to sit in a small chair, next to Hughie McCallum and Billy Anderson. There were girls too - Margaret Gray, Nan Galbraith - all starting school as well. But they all seemed to feel much more at home there than me; maybe I was still a bit of a mother's boy. Anyway, I have grateful memories of the way Margaret and Nan tried to make me more comfortable, but I was much too shy to talk to them.

At that time Buchanan School was in the building opposite the present-day school; it is now a private house. There were two teachers, Miss Johnstone for the younger children ages about five to eight. collectively known as the Wee Yins, and Mrs Black for the nine to eleven or twelve year olds known, logically, as the Big Yins, long before Billy Connolly took that title. The total number of pupils was probably between thirty and forty, although there was a temporary bulge due to an influx of short-term evacuees from Glasgow, during the bombing raids. We had gas-mask practice, I think on Mondays, when we all wore War Office issue gas masks for an hour or so, to ensure we knew the procedure in the event of a gas attack. I will never forget the suffocating feeling, and the smell of the rubber facemask, and I used to cheat by pulling it away from my cheek when the teacher wasn't watching.

John Macfarlane, June 2000, Buchanan School Reunion boat trip   *Photo: John Macfarlane*

The school's catchment area extended, as it still does, right up the Lochside to Rowardennan, and the school bus would pick up pupils from crofts such as the *Blair, Arrochymore, Cluan, Cashel, Woodburn, Sallochy,* and so on. Regulations prohibited pupils living less than three miles from school from using the bus, but leniency prevailed and I never had to walk the two miles to school, despite occasional growls from Duncan McLaren, the driver. The bus itself was a relic from the First World War, an ancient Albion chassis with a canvas roof that flapped in the wind. Its serial number was A2, but it soon acquired the nickname V2, in defiance of the German rockets that were causing destruction in London.

With many of the local able-bodied men away in the Forces, farmers were often short-handed and, every autumn, the children living on farms or crofts were allowed to take, I think, two weeks off school to assist in 'the tattie-howkin'. My family were in the boating business, which had no such emergency arrangements so I had to go to school as usual, although I remember there was a kind of relaxed atmosphere prevailing in school at those times. There was no electricity in the school, nor in most of the homes, until long after the War. Two open fireplaces served to heat the two classrooms, and lighting was provided by fishtail gas brackets. The acetylene gas was generated in the gas-shed at the back of the school, just on the banks of the Mar Burn.

The burn, although officially out of bounds, was accepted as part of our playground, and there were often wet feet in the classroom on summer afternoons. The Mains, a field downstream from the Sawmill, was our sports-ground, where various rough-and-tumble games were played, and the basic rules of fitba' were learnt.

Eventually, the eleven or twelve year-olds in Class Five (Year 7) sat the qualifying exams, and we duly went on to Balfron High School in August 1948, where I spent a further six years - but that's a story for another time.

Class IV, Balfron High School, 1951-52   *Photo: John Macfarlane*

When my brother and I were small, growing up in *Darach*, there were not many other children in the neighbourhood. Nearest, in *The Point*, were Margaret, Elizabeth and Duncan McLean. Across the field, in *Summerfield*, now called *Clairinch*, were Anne and Tommy Moffat. You had to go two miles to Milton of Buchanan to find other families with young kids, so we were a bit shy and uneasy in company when we started school. My aunts Cissie and Elsie, mother's twin sisters, lived with us for a while, and we felt they were like big sisters to us. Then across in *Violet Cottage* my aunt Jessie, father's sister, was like a nanny and spoiled us with sweeties, comics and other goodies. The

Boatyard, of course, was where I spent much of my time, and some of the folk who frequented there became for Barry and me, our best friends and acquaintances. Here I have to mention Angus MacFadyen, who started work with my grandfather in about 1947, became the regular skipper on the *Margaret*, and has remained a steadfast companion and friend until the present day.

Waterwitch **with the Inchfad mail, 1953. Angus MacFadyen with Alick Macfarlane.**
Photo: John Macfarlane

Salmon, it seems, were more plentiful in the Loch then, and every Saturday morning would see some ten or fifteen regular anglers setting up their rods and lines, before hiring a rowing boat and setting off for a day's fly-fishing. One of the most successful, in terms of fish caught and years of faithful attendance, was Ian Wood, whose book *Out from Balmaha* became a minor classic. Most of those regulars have gone on to the Anglers' Rest in the Sky, but the boats- *Heron, Lark, Whaup, Linnet, Kelpie* - are still going strong - some of them nearly eighty years old.

Salmon netting, Strathcashel Point, 1957. From left; Jack Gray (partly obscuring Duncan Mclean and Albert Sellar); Rab McLean; Barry Macfarlane; Peter Johnson; Willie Mclean; Alick Macfarlane; Donald Johnson. *Photo: John Macfarlane*

May 1945 brought spring, after a particularly frosty and snow-bound winter, and with it came Victory in Europe. There was a bonfire and celebrations in The Mains field, but no immediate change in rationing, and the air of austerity seemed to drag on for at least another five years. I finally believed that things were looking up when, in 1951, my father bought a NEW CAR! An Austin A70, which seemed to me, a restless fifteen-year-old, the ultimate in automotive achievement. A couple of years earlier, my father's new passenger launch, *Margaret*, had come into service. I spent all my spare time crewing on her on the Royal Mail run and general cruising, and developed an obsession with boats which, more than half-a-century later, I still haven't managed to shake off. *Margaret's* sister launches

(*Lady Jean, Marion, Waterwitch*,) also carried the mail at different times. There were two or three exceptionally cold winters then, and large areas in the southern end of the Loch were frozen hard. Regular boating was impossible, and the mail was transported on one occasion over the frozen Loch to the Islands on a sledge pulled by my father and Barry (that was actually some years later, in 1963). Of course, the local kids had a fabulous time skating and biking on the ice - not to mention the curling teams who held bonspiels that attracted players from surrounding districts for several weeks. Their curling stones were stored at the Boatyard from one winter to the next.

Allan Ferrie, Barry Macfarlane, and Angus MacFadyen at Balmaha Pier, 1957
Photo: John Macfarlane

Around that time, when I was maybe thirteen or fourteen years old, I was recruited by the Kirk Session to provide the motive power for the manually operated air-bellows on the Buchanan Church harmonium. I think Peter Johnson had also carried out this task before me. I soon knew most of the hymns and psalms off by heart, and no doubt sitting through the Rev F H 'Freddie' Fulton's sermons week after week had some beneficial effect. But at least I could boast that I earned some real pocket money, I think ten shillings per quarter, pumping the organ for Miss Bessie Stewart, and not many folk could say that.

Now for a look backwards. Always my grandfather would tell me: "in the Beginning, there were the Ancestors". They lived, worked and died on or near the Loch, and some of their gravestones are still to be seen in the old burial ground on Inchcailleach. In the Old Records of Stirling Commissary Court, there is the Will and Testament of *Alexander McFarlen of Coreclit in Inchecaulyoche parish* who died in 1657. I can't say for sure that he was 'one of ours', but I certainly know that my great-great-great grandfather Duncan lived on Inchfad in the 1750s, and his gravestone on Inchcailleach records the date of his death as 1783. He and his son John were in charge of a government distillery which was reputed to produce 'a liquor of great character and potency'. From Inchfad, Duncan, or perhaps one of his sons, ferried the barrels to the landing stage in Balmaha Bay. The owners of Inchfad to the present day have the right of access to this same landing stage.

From there, the cargo would be loaded onto horse-drawn delivery wagons, or transferred to sailing scows which then plied to Balloch and down the River Leven to bonded warehouses in Dumbarton. Later, my great-grandfather Alexander (1814-1880) continued the boating connection in the mid-1800s, and was contracted to transport roofing slates in a steam-driven scow from quarries at Sallochy and Luss to Balmaha for the Montrose Estates. From about 1895, the Duke's steam yacht *Violet* (there were actually two *Violet*s - the first one having been damaged by ice in 1897), was moored in and operated from Balmaha Bay. The gnarled timber piles, relics of the wharf from which the ducal family and their guests would board her, can still be seen in the Bay just in front of *Passfoot Cottage*, and remain as tangible links with Auld Lang Syne.

Invoice on Duke of Montrose for delivery to Balmaha of 44,400 slates at £2 per 1000; 15,600 small sized house slates at 14/- per 1000; 14,500 drain slates at 9/- per 1000. Total £106-4-10. Alexr. McFarlane signed receipt for £3-10-9d commission (8d in the £) at Catter on 18 January 1856.
Reproductions: John Macfarlane

Barry Macfarlane aboard *Margaret*, about 1970. *Photo: John Macfarlane*

***SS Violet* in Balmaha Bay, 1899.** *Photo: John Macfarlane*

Donald MacLean
Blairvockie

Donald MacLean at the top of Ben Lomond. *Photo: Chrissie Bannerman*

Donald MacLean left his native Harris in 1942 to serve in the Royal navy aged 18. After the war he joined the Merchant Navy but he never really liked being at sea. "I always had a notion for the shepherding." He became a shepherd with the Department of Agriculture in 1950. He married Catrìona Morrison in 1955 and they settled on the farms of Ben Lomond and Blairvockie, "where we spent thirteen good and happy years" before moving to Tyndrum. In 1980 he was awarded The Long Service Certificate and the B.E.M. Although officially retired and living at Thornhill, Donald, now aged 83, is still tending sheep and cattle daily.

FROM THE TOP OF BEN LOMOND
By Donald MacLean

From high Ben Lomond's peaks I've seen
The famous River Clyde
And down the Vale of Leven
And the wee hill of Duncryne.

The beautiful Strathendrick
Down by Drymen and Killearn
With the gentle flowing river
By Buchanan and Gartfairn.

Donald MacLean

Where it runs into Loch Lomond
The most famous loch of all
With its banks and braes so bonny
With the Bay at Balmaha.
There's a steamer leaves from Balloch
If you wish to go a sail
And it calls at Rowardennan
Then goes on to Inversnaid.

Then it's onwards to Ardlui
Where the mountains rise so high
And you're looking up Glenfalloch
And the road that leads to Skye.
There's an inn at Inverarnan
If you feel you need a 'dram'
Where the drovers held their cèilidhs
In the day that's long since gone.

You'll see the mighty Cobbler
Ben Vorlich and Ben Vane
And just across the water
There's the Falls of Inversnaid.
Craig Royston and the Ptarmigan
Beside the Shady Glen
And towering above them all
The Queen of Scottish Bens.

You can hear the mavis singing
You can hear the cuckoo's call
You can even see the prison
Of Rob Roy beside the shore.
The outlaw who stole the cattle
When he stayed up in Glengyle
And he's buried in Balquidder
Where they put him when he died.

Donald MacLean dressed for the Show.
Photo: Chrissie Bannerman

Now there's stories of Loch Lomond
Some are old and some are new
And some are told by fishermen
But they're not always true.
Of how they caught a salmon
And how many pounds it weighed
But there's never one as heavy
As the one that got away.

Donald MacLean

Now I'll add my own wee story
That I dearly love to tell
I met a big American
One day up on the Ben.
He asked if I liked whisky
And if I took a dram.
I said there's nothing better
I can think of for a man.

He said I've got a bottle
Of the stuff with me to-day
But on an empty stomach
It's not good for you they say.
But I said I think we'll risk it
For that statement could be true
For the less that's on your stomach
Then the quicker you get 'fu'.

We had a dram I thanked him
And he shook me by the hand
As he said 'I'm glad I met you
And you shared with me a dram'.
As I said, 'I fair enjoyed it
There's not many folk like you
That I meet up on Ben Lomond
With a drop of Mountain Dew'.

We shook hands and then we parted
And we went upon our way.
He was a rich American
And I was just a herd.
If he enjoyed the scenery
As I enjoyed his dram
He must have been quite happy
When we parted on the Ben.

Donald MacLean with his collies.
Photo: Chrissie Bannerman

Neil MacMillan
Rowardennan

Neil MacMillan is a weel kent face in Buchanan and well beyond. He has lived in the Parish all his life. He is a great person to have as a neighbour, always willing to lend a hand. He is also one of the best-known ceilidh dance musicians in Scotland.
Neil lives at Coille Mhor *with his wife Fiona. Daughters Sheena, Julie and Carol are now making their careers furth of Buchanan.*

Photo: Jenny Taggart

I want to write about one day from my childhood memories, round about 1965. The owner of Rowardennan Hotel at this time was Mr Kerr who through Stirling Council supplied transport to take the children who attended Balfron High School to link up with the service bus at Balmaha. The bus would then come back up the road to pick up the children who went to Buchanan Primary School, of which I was one. The one and only Dochie McLaren was the driver of this bus and stayed in a cottage behind the Hotel with his wife Lizzie and two daughters Betty and Joan. On his way back up the road I was picked up at the gate outside *Dubh Loch Cottage* where I stayed with my mum and dad, big brother Peter and sisters Jan, Mary, Chrissie and Grace. Dochie took me to the Hotel petrol pump, which was beside where the telephone box is now, then he would go for his breakfast. I would fill the bus with fuel from the petrol pump which was worked with a hand pump. The number for the safety padlock was 111 (this was my big secret with Dochie).

Once finished I would feed the pigs which the Hotel kept for their own use. At this time a generator powered the electricity for the Hotel, which I filled with a hand pump from drums of diesel beside the generator. When I was finished Dochie would limp up the hill towards the generator shed and shout, "Time to go, come and get yer hands washed" - which I did - and then got my treat from Dochie. One sweetie!

Neil MacMillan

The one and only Dochie McLaren. *Photo: Willie Simpson*

Back on the bus I would take my seat by the door, as I was Dochie's door boy, and head for the first pickup who was Mavis Savage at the Youth Hostel. Then we picked up Dochie's daughter Joan, my older sister Chrissie and on to the Forestry cottages where we picked up one girl and eleven boys.

Further down the road we picked up Andy and Nan Simpson at Cashel Farm, Sheena McLaren at *Critreoch*, Ann and Roy Taylor at *The Blair*, Christopher Morton at Milarrochy Campsite, the Robertsons at *Arrochymore*, the Johnstons at *Passfoot*, John Frier at *Balmaha House*, and the last pickup before getting to school was Gavin Shanks at Auchingyle Farm.

The teachers at this time were Mr Sinclair who replaced Miss Pew as head teacher and Miss McLaren.

I spent most of my primary school time in the original school, which was beside the schoolhouse. In June 1967 the new school was opened across the road. The late Mrs Mary Donaldson was the school cleaner, and in the mornings I would have a blether with her before she went home. Mrs Forbes was our dinner lady and would cook our school dinners for us, and later it was Mrs Gilmore.

There always seemed to be things happening in and around that time and these events always seemed big. On this particular day I and a group of other boys were down at the Mar Burn stepping-stones during dinner break. Now this was territory forbidden by the teachers as it was out of bounds and we knew it. This was the day that Duncan MacFadyen, the brother of Angus MacFadyen local boat builder, came home from working abroad, flying an aeroplane. We were climbing up the chestnut tree, which always had a good crop, when we saw this plane crossing over and heading in the Conich Hill direction. We thought it was just great but carried on throwing down and picking up as many chestnuts as we could.

Then out of the blue this plane flew right over the tree and I thought we've been caught stealing chestnuts. We all made a dash for the stepping stones to run back up the field when just at that moment the plane flew over the village of Buchanan, over the edge of the Sawmill, where Duncan's house is now, and landed in the field right beside us. We all thought, "That's it - we've been well and truly caught". We hesitated for a moment or two, then the cockpit of the plane opened slowly and this person got out. It was William Gilmore who recognised the person as Duncan MacFadyen and I can tell you we were all very relieved. We headed back to the school to tell the head teacher Mr Sinclair of our excitement, forgetting that we shouldn't have been at the Mar Burn in the first place. We all got a row but we still had our chestnuts. That night, at home, I retold all that had happened to mother and father.

Neil's mother and father, Janet and Neil MacMillan. *Photo: Willie Simpson*

At this time at the *Dubh Loch* we had no electricity or telephone so in the evenings after dinner I would help father with any jobs, like feeding the dogs, or chores that needed doing around the house.

I enjoyed building things for myself like bogies or bicycles and watching father as he worked on a car. I learned a lot from that. I once made a barrow from old pram wheels and a wooden box which I put handles on to. I would fill it with chips from the roadsides and gravel paths around the house. I also would go to the bay, where the University Field Station is now, to bail out father's and Johnnie Galbraith's clinker-built boats. This was an important job and I knew I had to do it properly.

Later in the evening I'd play a few tunes on my accordion or mouth organ before heading off to bed.

Lisbeth McCaig
Buchanan Castle

Lisbeth McCaig, née Russell, and her husband live in Drymen. They have two daughters who are both married, and now have three grandsons.

I came to Buchanan Castle when I was about ten years of age. I do remember we had a great time there as children. When we first came to *Tor Mhor*, the old isolation block of the hospital, all the doors for the individual rooms were blue and some still had the patient's names on them and there were little stoves in the corridors to heat the old hospital (must have been a bit chilly). I think my parents were one of the first families to purchase one of the old hospital buildings, although I do remember Air Commodore Primrose (of the monocle!) being there before us up at the Castle.

I can't remember exactly when the Castle roof was blown up, but prior to that the building was opened and the interior fittings and panelling were sold off. My father bought central heating radiators, which he himself fitted in our house. My brother David and I had a great time during the selling off period as we would go and wander through the Castle and up to the top tower just below the Highlander statue – great views. A lot of the other hospital buildings were being sold at this time and I ashamed to say we children (mainly Fergusons and Russells) kind of ransacked the empty ones and even got rid of the wee stoves and blackout curtains and made huts where we had hours of fun up behind our house. We also nearly set the place on fire at one point! The pond down at High Mains and the Ice House were of interest as was the old well at the junction of the road going down to the Golf Club.

Buchanan Castle in its heyday.   *Photo: Arthur Bayfield*

Our summer holidays were spent playing in these huts making rafts for the newt pond (as we called it) behind Miss Gladys Beckett's house. We also explored the Estate up to the grotto at the Duchess's Bridge and the dog's graveyard and climbed over the arch of the suspension bridge - what a thought now that I am old. I can also remember the old railway line; I think they kept wartime stuff there. Davy McNaughton looked after the gardens and I remember going into the big glasshouses where one could buy peaches and vegetables from the walled garden. The Home Farm was also functioning then and we collected our milk in cans from Mrs McGill.

Eventually a lot of the old buildings that were not sold were demolished and new houses were built. It was amazing how many long corridors there were joining some of the houses to the Castle itself. Our next-door neighbours were Stewart and Muriel Watt, a lovely couple who were very good to us children, taking us out on the Loch in their boat called *Nuala* (I think). Across the road were the four Ferguson children. They used their house as a holiday house at first and David and I used to look across hoping they were coming out for the weekend. Eventually, of course, they moved here permanently. They then purchased another hospital building and turned it into a battery hen house. I can still remember the noise from all the hens when we went in. John Ronald and his wife, or maybe it was the Maitlands, I can't remember, looked after the hens. I don't know how long the battery hen project lasted but eventually the hen house was turned into three houses and the Ferguson's themselves moved into one, selling their original house to Dr Doug Weldon, his wife Sue, and their five daughters.

In the early days everyone knew everyone else and the parents did a lot of work on their homes themselves - not like nowadays. My father made the road up to *Tor Mhor* with Bill Maitland from Buchanan Smiddy. Before there were too many people living there - I think it was at New Year - everyone congregated at a party. I remember going to the Ferguson's original *Langcroft* and the Adam's house, now called *Sprawlie* and owned by the Bruces, and there was even dancing to records on the brown linoleum hospital floors. This only happened in the early days and eventually the Feuers Ball was started and took place at the Golf Club for a good many years.

One of the few things I do regret is that my parents did not send us to Balfron High School. My father was travelling in and out to Glasgow to work every day and I think it was decided just to leave David and I at our town schools - a great pity as I feel now we would have got to know far more people in Drymen of our own age. When we went to school we cycled down the avenue for the 7.40 am bus and left our bikes in a shed at the *Lodge* gates. I remember a family called Cuthbertson and when their children started school they had to walk by themselves all the way to Buchanan Primary - quite something for five year olds. It would never happen nowadays. We did, however, go to Sunday School at Buchanan and even continued going to Bible class with Mr Fulton at *The Manse*. We were also in the Nativity play

Life at the Castle is quite different nowadays. There are lots of expensive houses and I do not think I would like to live there now. My parent's house was the last of the old hospital buildings to have the asbestos roof replaced. This happened when the house was sold and the couple who stay there now are only the second residents of the Isolation Block.

Alice McIntyre and Jeanetta Doherty
Milton of Buchanan

Alice, who lives in Milton of Buchanan, worked for the Royal Bank in Drymen for nine years. She was then transferred to Glasgow working in various Branches until her early retirement in 2003. She now works in the Balmaha Visitors Centre in the summer months. During winter 2006/07 she worked in The Village Shop in Drymen.

Photo: Jenny Taggart

As a twenty-one year old, Jeanetta worked for a Stockbroker in London. She returned to Scotland and worked in the Royal Bank for five years, although not at the same time as her sister Alice - close relatives working together was against bank rules! She then worked with BAA at Glasgow Airport, where daughter Louise now works. Currently, she is an administrator at Buchanan Castle Golf Club.

Photo: Jenny Taggart

Alice McIntyre and Jeanetta Doherty

Alice lived at Buchanan Smithy for the first two years of her life but Jeanetta was born in the house that she still lives in at Creityhall Road, Milton of Buchanan. Alice now lives close-by in Creityhall Drive.

We were two of the first generation of children who moved into, or were born in the houses built in Milton of Buchanan by Stirling County Council in 1949. The houses were supposed to be temporary post war houses and were very basic. The gardens, which had been left basically a field, had to be cultivated and I believe most of the grass seed came from Fulton Ronald down at the farm.

Creityhall Road, Milton of Buchanan. *Photo: James Taggart*

As children, we were very well looked after although we didn't have a lot of money. All of our parents worked on the land and were extremely clever with the means they had at their disposal. Almost all of the basic vegetables were grown and harvested by each family. Other supplies were bought from various vans which had weekly round to The Milton and outlying areas; Brown the butcher; the Co-op and the Dempsters sold groceries; there was a baker's van and a fish van plus others. Every night, in summer at any rate, we children went down to the farm with our milk cans to get milk. We would go to the byre and watch the cows being milked by Minnie and Fulton Ronald, and then the milk was taken to the milk parlour for processing through filters before our cans were filled. We also got our eggs at the farm.

Alice McIntyre and Jeanetta Doherty

The farm and surrounding fields and burns and the Sawmill were our main play areas. We were always welcomed at the farm by the Ronald family. We would sometimes help Minnie with her hens. She used to go down a long flight of stairs at the back of the farmhouse and across the burn to two henhouses she had up beside the top burn.

School reunion, Alice and Mary Donaldson.
Photo: Jim Bennett

Reunion, Jeanetta and Ronnie McLaren
Photo: Jim Bennett

The two burns down from the back of our houses are where we spent a lot of our time. Whether looking for tadpoles, just jumping back and forward across it or negotiating the reeds, we were easily pleased. We knew about kinds of trees, wildflowers, insects and birds and the ways of the countryside. We also spent a lot of time down at the Mar Burn, which was much bigger. Again, we loved negotiating our way across the stones starting maybe at *Gartincaber Cottage* where Jean and Carol Sellars stayed; if you fell in you waited until you dried out before going home. We would come down to the Mill Bridge which we sometimes sat under and listened for anything going over it, and it was exciting if anything actually did, and then climb up the side of the bridge. When I look at it now, it seems really scary. We would also play hide and seek in the rhododendrons on the banks beside the school. As the Meal Mill was no longer in use we also used to play up in the dam. The trees and beech hedges were also great fun. We spent lots of time climbing the trees and the hedges could be anything you wanted them to be, being just a seat or a hidey-hole. Sometimes on a Sunday afternoon Mr Hughie Forbes would take a lot of us across the fields bird spotting which again was great fun. Apart from really wet days and winter nights, as children we were hardly ever indoors.

Another thing we used to do was plant potatoes at Gartfairn for Willie and Mrs Ronald and also at The Milton for Minnie and Hughie Ronald. In the autumn we went tattie howking to lift the potatoes. It was hard work and good fun because you were with your pals, but the highlight, for me at least, was the picnics we had. The baskets would be brought full of sandwiches and cakes and drinks for all of us.

One evening a week we got the bus down to Drymen to go to the Brownies. First stop was Bilsland's shop, which was opposite the Clachan, where we got our supply of sweets before going to the Church Hall in Stirling Road. Jenny Johnston and Rosemary Howe ran the Brownies. We did lots of activities including learning to tie knots, semaphore and playing games. In the summer we sometimes went out for nature walks around Drymen.

On Saturday morning Alice and I went along to Bessie Stewart at *Taynunich* in Balmaha for piano lessons. Bessie was a great teacher and she played the organ in the church. She had a spaniel called Speed and while one of us had a piano lesson, the other got to play with Speed who devoured everything in sight including our mitts and scarves.

We attended Buchanan School, which is now a private house. In the 1950s Miss Jessie Macfarlane was the infant teacher and Miss Alice Ewan (who died last year) taught primary 4-7 classes. I also remember being taught by John K Sinclair when I was in the older classroom. We had a visiting PE teacher, Mr Mercer, and for music we used to go over the road to the lunch room to listen to the radio programme *Singing Together*. Arriving at school, the cloakrooms with pigeonholes were inside the main door. The toilets were at the rear of the building. I think most people enjoyed being at Buchanan School, this was evident at a school reunion we had in 2000.

Buchanan School reunion, 2000. A few intrepid souls opted for a cruise on the Loch from Balmaha Boatyard. *Photo: Jim Bennett*

Alice McIntyre and Jeanetta Doherty

The only thing we didn't like about school was the arrival of the milk lorry every day. The bottles were usually dirty, some with the dung still on, and in particular in winter the milk would be frozen and would be put near radiators to thaw out - I still can't drink milk to this day. Also, across the road were the Museum and a large playshed which was a bit like a pavilion, and also the sundial, which had been gifted to the parish by the minister, a Rev McKenzie, I think, and which is now up in the churchyard. We were allowed to play almost anywhere in those days. There was little traffic back in the fifties and so in the break we could cross the road to play in the rhododendrons and in the playshed. At Easter we would roll our Easter eggs down the hill beside the playshed. In the early 1960s Mrs Sinclair, the head teacher's wife, ran a Scottish country dance class in the present school, which we went along to one evening a week.

On Sundays we went to Church. From an early age we attended Sunday School taken by Mrs Mary Donaldson. We always wore our Sunday clothes, which were special. We were presented with Bibles and other books from Rev Fulton for perfect attendance. Most of us were christened in Buchanan Church and the Rev Fulton added all our names to the Cradle Roll in the Church. Later on in our lives when Rev Ian Gray was the minister we became members of the Church and attended our classes in the evening in the Vestry.

Around 1959/60 Stirling Council built another eight houses and a block of four flats making what is Creityhall Drive, where Alice now lives. We had previously had a set of swings adjacent to our house at the top of the road, but because of the new buildings a swing park with a roundabout was made at the bottom of Creityhall Drive.

In our teens we attended Balfron High School. At weekends we worked locally. Alice worked in the Winnock Hotel in Drymen learning to cook with Mr and Mrs Agnew. Jeanetta worked at Passfoot Tearoom as a waitress for Jimmy and Molly Johnston.

We had a very happy childhood here in Buchanan, I think mainly due to the fact that everyone who lived here was like part of a big family. There are lots more happy memories which would take forever to cover but I'm sure have been mentioned by our friends who grew up here.

Nothing like a reunion to get the tongues going.   *Photo: Jim Bennett*

Elsie McKinlay
Gartfairn Farm

Elsie McKinlay (Elsie Barbour) was born and lived in Gartfairn farm in the 1920s and 1930s. Her father, James Barbour, then moved with his family from Gartfairn to Machribeg farm in Southend, Kintyre, where Elsie worked on the farm for several years. She married Dan McKinlay and set up home in Campbeltown, where she still lives in the same neighbourhood near her daughters and grand-children.

Photo: Elsie McKinlay

My father James Barbour moved to Gartfairn Farm in Buchanan Parish from Southend, Kintyre, early in the 20th century. My earliest memories of my life in Gartfairn were when my twin sister Cissie and I were about three we had scarlet fever and were taken to Lennoxtown Fever Hospital. Later on, we would walk with our older sister Minnie every day to Buchanan School, as did lots of other scholars. I remember playing hide-and-seek amongst the bushes and shrubs around the school, and also we went down to the Mar Burn to catch tadpoles in jam-jars, sometimes falling in, not a popular pastime by teachers' standards. Our teachers were Miss Jessie Macfarlane and Miss Jean Spittal. The Headmaster was Mr Ballantyne.

Our nearest neighbours were the Rev Walter Lacey and family in *The Manse*, the Purdie family at *Auchmar*, Mr and Mrs Retson and their daughter Nessie in *Gartincaber*, Mr and Mrs Ballantyne and their niece Betty Pringle in *The Schoolhouse*. Even though we all left the area long ago, we remained friends all our days.

On the farm, I remember having to help thinning the turnips. I hated every minute, Feeding calves was a chore which I liked. Summer holidays, which were always sunny, were spent often with our school friends coming to Gartfairn, or us visiting them.

Miss Jean Spittall and Miss Jessie Macfarlane, teachers at Buchanan School, about 1920.   *Photo: Elsie McKinlay*

All my cousins would come from Kintyre to visit us and the highlight of their holiday was having a big family picnic on one of the islands on Loch Lomond. A fire would be lit, potatoes boiled to be eaten with mince, and garden pears consumed for dessert. Drinking water was taken straight from the Loch on the way - all very simple pleasures. My brother-in-law Alick Macfarlane would take us to the island and bring us back. I think his boat at that time was named *Duchess of York*.

The special event of our school year was the Christmas party given by the Duke and Duchess of Montrose at *Buchanan Castle*. It was a fairyland to us children - the beautifully lit tree, and being entertained with a Punch and Judy show in the Castle. I still treasure one of the presents the Duchess gave me. Another event that stands out in my memory was the Silver Jubilee of King George V and Queen Mary. There were school sports and in the evening a bonfire and fireworks. Some over-enthusiastic revellers set the heather on the Conich alight.

I am sure the district will have changed in many ways, but I keep in touch with my nephew John Macfarlane, and memories of my childhood in Buchanan are very dear to me.

Duncan McAlpine, ploughman at Gartfairn farm, about 1920. Duncan and his wife came from Kintyre. He was later employed by Stirling County Council as a roadman in the Buchanan area. *Photo: Elsie McKinlay*

Buchanan School, pupils and teachers, about 1930. Elsie and Cissie Barbour (centre of 2nd row); Miss Spittal and Miss Macfarlane, (Left and right ends of 3rd row.) *Photo: Elsie McKinlay*

Duncan McLean
Gartincaber Cottage

Duncan McLean and his wife Shona live in Kettering, Northamptonshire. They have three grandchildren: their son, who lives in Dubai has one son; their daughter, who was married in Buchanan Church, has two, a girl and a boy and they live in Bath.

Duncan retired from Travis Perkins over three years ago where he was Group Transport Manager and has set up his own consultancy business, still in the Transport Industry.

Photo: John Macfarlane

My mother and father Willie and Meg were married in Buchanan Church in 1933. In 1935, my oldest sister Margaret was born at *Auchengyle*. Some time before 1938 my mother and father moved to the *Home* (now *Montrose House*) where my sister Elizabeth was born. War must have started when they were at the *Home* as when the children from Clydebank were being evacuated my parents ended up with over thirty children. I am not sure how long this lasted but at some time between the start of the war and August 1940 they moved to *Gartincaber Cottage*, which had just been built. My father worked for the Duke and in addition to working on the Estate he drove the Duke to the various meetings he was involved in during the war.

I started at Buchanan School while we lived in *Gartincaber Cottage*. I remember walking to school with Margaret and Elizabeth. The school in the 1940s was small, only two classes. The only classmates I remember are Effie Anderson, Anna Shaw, Fulton Ronald, Alex McLaren and Tommy Moffat. Our teacher was Jennie Johnston (Jennie Longlegs) the other teacher was, as I remember, Chrissie Ewan (Crabbit Chrissie).

I have no real memories of school other than I remember the highlight of the week was when the baker's van stopped outside the school and the pupils were allowed to buy something. Shiny topped buns were a favourite; they cost a halfpenny each. In the winter the school was heated by two coal fires, one at each end of the school. Alex McLaren and

I were caught throwing laurel leaves on the fire, which sparked and hissed to the great annoyance of the teacher.

As a family we moved to Balmaha from *Gartincaber Cottage* in 1946 and for a few years lived in *The Point*. In 1948 we moved from Balmaha to the east of Stirlingshire.

Balmaha from *The Point*.   *Photo: John Macfarlane*

Like the other children from Balmaha and those from up the Pass we travelled to school in the school bus. It was old, green, with wooden seats, driven by Duncan McLaren and owned by Tom Kerr of Rowardennan Hotel.

I remember once (must have 1947), when there was a lot of snow the bus could not run because of snowdrifts - so no school. Jack Gray drove a tractor with a snowplough and cleared the road. Barry Macfarlane, Tommy Moffat and I followed the tractor along the road as far as the Church and watched the Buchanan children in the playground before walking back to Balmaha.

Jack Gray clearing snow on the Balmaha road; Ronnie Johnson and Dan Currie on the tractor.
Photo: Ronnie Johnson

In the wood, between the Church and the road into *The Manse*, there were small corrugated shelters with boxes of ammunition stored. I am not sure who was responsible for this ammunition but I do remember that American soldiers passed the school in trucks and we would stand on the railings and shout to the solders as they passed: "any gum chum?" They did give us kids chewing gum.

Ann Moffat, older sister of Tommy Moffat, was knocked down out side the school by one of the American trucks as she ran out of the gate to get on the school bus. She was stunned, but otherwise uninjured and recovered quickly.

Sunday School was an important part of local life. Two things stick in my mind. Dear Mary McAlpine trying to control and teach the children, and in one very early Nativity play the younger children were dressed up as angels. Fulton Ronald and I, among the unlikely angels, got into a bit of a squabble behind the scenes during the performance.

Balmaha was a great place to live; the late and missed Barry Macfarlane and I were the best of pals and remained so until Barry's death.

At the end of the war Loch Lomond had two steamers, the *Princess May* and *Prince Edward*, which plied the Loch with day-trippers. Passengers would get a train from Glasgow and get the steamer at Balloch. The first stop was Balmaha and dozens, if not hundreds, would get off at the pier and make their way to the sandy shore passed the Macfarlane's Boatyard. As they passed *Passfoot Cottage* where there was a small shop, they would stock up with bottles of lemonade. I am not sure why, but they seldom collected up the empty lemonade bottles. Barry and I would collect the bottles and return them to *Passfoot* over the following weeks and months in sufficient numbers that allowed us to get lemonade for ourselves without money, by using the one-penny bottle deposits.

Barry and I got into trouble once - well many times. The occasion I remember was we found an old canvas boat in the old boathouse and set off for *Passfoot*. It turned out that the boat was not leak proof and by the time we got to the *Passfoot* side it was nearly full of water. Not daunted, we empted out the water, got our bottles of lemonade and set off back to the Boatyard side. Not sure why, but the boat filled up again.

Winters were colder and we always had snow. Loch Lomond would freeze and when the roads were clear dozens of skaters would find their way to the ice. One skater I remember was Fritz, a German prisoner of war who worked with the Ronalds at Gartfairn Farm. He was a great skater; he could skate as fast backwards as he could forwards.

1947 was the year I started skating, Angus MacFadyen put on my skates and carried me down to the ice. That year we skated and sledged by lamplight.

Buchanan ladies on the ice, 1947
Photo: John Macfarlane

Duncan McLean

I remember that year skating round to the mouth of the River Endrick. The ice had frozen in the river. Not only was it frozen, it had curled up the banks to give a curved skating surface like today's skateboard parks. Also, I never knew why, but there was a gap in the ice between Inchcailleach and the pier that ran all the way to the mouth of the Endrick that opened and closed morning and night with a great roar.

I am now living in England, but when I am in Scotland I still return to Buchanan and Balmaha - places of very happy and sad memories.

Duncan McLean and *Lady Jean* on the ice, 1947.   *Photo: John Macfarlane*

Duncan McLean lived at *Gartincaber Cottage*, 1940-46.   *Photo: Carol Cameron*

Flora McPherson
Milton of Buchanan

Flora McPherson spent a lifetime looking after others. Now she is enjoying a well-earned rest at her home in Milton of Buchanan. Although not in the best of health, she is able to live alone enjoying the company of friends and neighbours.

Photo: Jenny Taggart

My name is Flora McPherson. I was born on the Island of Islay; I was an only child and lived on the island for my first two years. My father was a shepherd and moved around several estates during my childhood. We went from Islay to Campbeltown and then to the Isle of Arran where I began my schooling at Sliddery School. From there we went to Loch Awe, on to Luing Island and finally in 1953 to Old Manse Farm at Balmaha. My father worked for Mr J M Bannerman, who later became Lord Bannerman, where he stayed until he retired.

I had finished school by the time we moved to this area and I went to work at Balmaha Tearoom for Donald Maclean. It was situated on the Lochside opposite what is now The Highland Way Hotel. The Tearoom was open during the summer months and was very busy; coaches came from Edinburgh as well as increasing numbers of cars. Some people would go on boat trips around the Islands on the Loch.

Mr Maclean also owned the petrol pumps and shops across the road from the Tearoom. There was also a small shop, actually a wooden hut, which sold groceries and newspapers. Before he acquired the hut he sold groceries from his home at *Balmaha House*. He would simply open one of the bedroom windows to make a sale.

I worked at the Tearoom for six years before moving to work at the Rowardennan Hotel. My cousin Cathy was already working there so I decided to join her. Mr Thomas Kerr owned the Hotel. I was waitress, barmaid and generally did any jobs needed. This included serving in the little shop at the Hotel on occasion, serving sweets, ice cream and soft drinks.

The Hotel was very busy during the summer as quite a few people came to walk up Ben Lomond. They came by car and by steamer from Balloch. Mr Duncan McLaren was employed to collect pier dues from the passengers. We would watch the passengers leaving the ferry so that we could judge how busy we were going to be serving afternoon teas.

We also had local customers. The two shepherds from Blairvockie, Donald MacLean (not the Donald Maclean of the Balmaha Tearoom) and Donald McDermott, would call in when rounding up sheep. They would herd the sheep into the Hotel car park and leave the sheep dogs in charge outside while they enjoyed a few drinks in the bar. The sheep never moved.

The two Donalds, MacLean (left) and McDermott (right) with a wee sensation at Hogmanay.
Photo: Chrissie Bannerman

The locals also had a great time attending dances after the Buchanan Sheepdog Trials, and at Christmas and New Year, although most people went home before the bells at New Year. The staff came from all around the local area: Gartocharn, Alexandria and Renton. They travelled on the bus as far as Balmaha and then would be picked up by the Hotel car.

During this time I lived with my parents at *Arrochymore*. My father retired from shepherding when he found walking up to thirty miles a day on the hills became too much as he got older. He then worked in forestry. Initially we had to move to the Arrochar Hotel before moving to live at *Woodburn Cottage*. My father also worked for Mr McAuley at Cashel Farm. We lived at *Blair Cottage* during that time.

Flora McPherson

Blair Cottage, 2007   *Photo: James Taggart*

Various owners came and went at the Hotel and I decided to have a change of scene. I moved into domestic service and worked for a lot of local people, including housekeeper to Mrs Russell-Ferguson at *Sallochy* for about a year and Mrs Finlay at Blairvockie Farm, which was very busy. They had cattle and sheep on Ben Lomond, and actually built the hill road up from the farm. Their son Ewan also ran a pony trekking business. I worked for Mrs Blossom at Balmaha, and at *West Lodge* - first for Mrs Paisley and later for Mrs Satterthwaite. I spent some time with Mrs Craik helping with the B&B at *Lomond Bank*. Finally I spent six years working for the Minister, Mr Hay, and his wife at *The Manse*.

As soon as we moved into the Buchanan area my mother and I joined the WRI, which was held in the Memorial Hall at Milton of Buchanan. I remained a member until it sadly closed last year. I helped with the famous rural teas at the Rural and the Flower Show throughout the years of my membership. I was on the committee and distributed the Rural magazines. I really enjoyed the outings and activities. We did a show based on the TV programme *Take the High Road*. I played a small girl going into the shop. Mrs Hay played Isabel Blair the shopkeeper.

I lived with my parents until their deaths, my mother in 1968 and father in 1977. I moved into my house here in The Milton on the 16th September 1978. I am very happy here although I had to retire from work when I was sixty because of ill health.

I now have very poor vision but with help from family and friends I keep up to date with local events with the Talking Book Service, the Stirling Observer on tape, and with radio and television. The houses around me have all changed hands. I really miss Margaret Campbell who was a great friend and neighbour, but it is nice to see young families coming into the area.

I am able to get out and about. My cousin takes me shopping and neighbours give me a lift to and from Church and to the Guild and Senior Citizens meetings. I have help from Personal Carers each day and from a District Nurse when needed.

The 'Buchanan Ladies' are trying to carry on some of the Rural traditions by arranging outings and meals. I enjoy taking part in these and I do hope they continue. I still attend the Buchanan Flower Show each August. I now go as a guest and it is real treat to be served with my tea instead of always doing the serving.

Dig that crazy Rural band. *Photo: Willie Simpson*

Flower Shows prizes. Left to right: Mrs Hay, Margaret Simpson (President), Sheena McAllister, George Cummine. *Photo: Willie Simpson*

Hermione Thornhill
Auchmar

Hermione Thornhill is the daughter of the eighth Duke and Duchess of Montrose. She was born at Auchmar and spent her childhood in Buchanan Parish. She moved to Glasgow recently where her husband lectures at the University of Glasgow. Hermione is a clinical psychologist. The Thornhills have twins, Grace and John.

Photo: Catherine Montrose

I grew up in *Auchmar*, the house my great-grandparents built when they could no longer live in Buchanan Castle. I spent my first two years in *The Garden Flat*, a self-contained annexe to the main house, which was let out. This was where my mum and dad lived, when they were first married, after they returned from their winter wedding in Ottawa, Canada in early 1970. I think I was probably pretty pleased with myself by the time I was two years old. I look very cheery in photographs, though I am usually modelling some fairly horrendous head-gear: large woolly hats in winter and voluminous cotton inventions which look like large billowing upturned pants in summer. The garden at *Auchmar* was ideal for small children to sit on rugs in summer or keep cool in a paddling pool. And in winter there was always snowmen and sledging.

Family lore has it that the bliss of my existence was shattered in August 1973, when my brother Jamie was born. Apparently, though of course there is no hard evidence to support this, I was insanely jealous that I was no longer the sole recipient of the adult attention quota for small people. I threw an impressive scene at his christening, successfully vandalising my parents' bedroom and my new velvet dress with large quantities of talcum powder. I am sure it seemed to me then (as I recall I also felt about my second brother Ronnie's christening two years later) that it really was quite unjust and really a waste that a tiny baby, who couldn't possibly have any use for such objects, should be showered with gifts of books, silver, and things that sparkled. And to add insult to injury, when I attempted to reach out to these creatures in sisterly affection and with a view to becoming involved in their nurture, I was reprimanded and told firmly by an extremely - to me, at least - austere maternity nurse who seemed to be around on a twenty-four hour basis, "Don't touch baby's bottle" and certainly "don't go within five feet of a dirty nappy"!

So with the birth of Jamie we moved into the main part of *Auchmar*: *The Garden Flat* and *The Top Flat* were let out, along with *The Bothy* and *High Auchmar*. Quite a few of my childhood memories are to do with the fun we used to have with the various tenants who lived next to us at different times. I am not sure they realised when they signed the contract that it would involve being permanently harassed by three children, but they soon found out.

First, there was Major Ryan. We believed he was a military hero of some sort and he may well have been. At any rate, he was something to do with the Parachute Regiment and certainly owned a large parachute, which he used to spread out on the lawn to check from time to time. As children we thought this a magnificent sight. Often when we came back from school, Major Ryan would be outside his garage covered in grease, tending to his beloved motorbike. Jamie would sometimes 'help out' which mainly involved also getting covered in grease, and he also gave us rides down to Balmaha and back which, for a seven year old, is about as good as things could get. The poor man was also regularly drafted into pillow-fights (at which he was very good) and looking back I just hope he wasn't in the throes of trying to recover from some major military operation every time he hung out with us and we bombarded him with pillows and demands for drinks and snacks.

Then there was Miss Garety, I think quite a talented artist. However the poor woman had to put up with being the object of some social disapproval due to her habit of sometimes drinking more than she could take (as an artist must) and keeping male company which contravened the local mores set by John Knox in the 1500s and generally loyally adhered to since. She once offered to teach me sculpture but I am ashamed to say I was a very poor student and regret not taking this offer more seriously. As it was, she made a lovely sculpture of clay for me, which sadly broke after a few years when it fell off a mantlepiece. She also did many paintings, some inspired by the garden at *Auchmar*, in particular the river and waterfall, but I have no idea what became of her or them.

Individuals and families came and went: Mrs Powell only after she had plied us all with a thousand glasses of Coke and hundreds of Kit Kats, and walked up and down the drive keeping fit each day for many years; Brian Cant and his sons after scores of games of Cowboys and Indians; the Durnins and Turnbulls after widely celebrated late-night parties at *High Auchmar*.

Apart from those in the immediate vicinity, our social life mainly revolved around classmates at Buchanan School in those days. We started at the Nursery, where I remember a large array of toys and singing games like 'The Farmer's in his Dell'. It was fun waiting to see if you would be picked to be the farmer or the wife or the child or the dog but you dreaded being the bone because you knew that everyone would thump you energetically at "the bone won't break"!

Jamie Graham, far right, rehearses for School concert, Christmas 1983.
Photo: Chrissie Bannerman

Buchanan School, 1983. Ronnie Graham is in the second row, third from the right.
Photo: Chrissie Bannerman

There were eight of us in our class and ours was the biggest class: Helen McAllister, Aileen Findlay, Lorna Hay, Andrew Ronald, Dickson Jackson, Mark Cummine, Alasdair

Thomson and me. I think Anna-Maria Poci was in our class for a while as well, when her family ran the ice cream and fish and chip shop in Balmaha. There were two classrooms: one for Primary 1-2 and one for Primary 3-7. Mrs Leiper used to divide the blackboard up into sections and make a list of what each class should work their way through that morning or afternoon. I think most year groups consisted of less than five children. Sometimes Chrissie Bannerman would take the class for Gaelic lessons. I've lost count of the number of times I had to leave the room, knock on the door, come in, be asked how I was, and accept a cup of tea with milk and sugar! *Tapadh leibh.*

School was in some ways very different to how it is now. Playtimes, for example, were completely unregulated then: there were no playground assistants and no one had ever heard of an anti-bullying policy. It was pretty much a free-for-all. Considering this, I guess we all conducted ourselves reasonably well. There was plenty of petty bickering, cliques, and low-level bullying but I think violence was quite rare. We played 'white horses', 'kiss chase', 'kiss cuddle or torture', football, skipping, jumping over various arrangements of elastic bands and 'what's the time Mr Wolf?' Tag was probably one of the simplest and most popular games and when we all knew the rhymes too well so that we knew where to stand so as not to be 'It', Mark Cummine invented a new rhyme so that no-one could cheat. I still remember it and it went like this: 'eeny meeny zicka zacka papalouski een tabacka een skeen boxaleen eenie meenie blossom'. If you were pointed at on 'blossom' you weren't 'It' until the last person was left.

If there was any trouble in the playground, the teachers didn't really want to know about it. I remember Mrs Leiper saying to me when I knocked on the staff room door one break time, "I'm trying to drink my coffee and I don't want to be disturbed unless Andrew Ronald is hanging upside down from a second story window by his knees". Considering the school was only built on one story, this was a fairly unlikely occurrence. However the perpetrators of any misdemeanours who were discovered after break-time (usually this involved some kind of trouble in the boys toilets) could look forward to the belt or a few smacks on the palm with a ruler for minor offences.

Sometimes after school or at the weekends we would go to each other's houses and this was a great adventure. I remember going to *Blairvockie* with Aileen, with whom I think I had some kind of love-hate relationship, and having a great time riding ponies there. We also experimented, aged seven, with Aileen's sister's tampax, trying to figure out what on earth they were meant for. Aileen had a fairly good idea but it was all still pretty baffling. We did our first Brownie badge at Aileen's, mixing up an instant cake-mix for our cookery badge, which seemed quite ridiculous to us who had been baking 'proper' cakes for years. At my house we did a lot of dressing up with various cast-offs of my mum, aunts and grandmother. We would pretend to have tea and also put on brief theatrical productions.

Birthday parties were also great events and I remember very clearly Lorna Hay having a party, it must have been about her sixth or seventh. At any rate, *Grease* had just come out and we danced all afternoon to the sound track which her parents had on an LP and ate jelly and ice cream. I still think of that when my daughter watches *Grease* and sings along to *Summer Loving* now.

In the febrile world of my childish imagination my heart was won and broken ten times by the age of eight. I think they said of Audrey Hepburn that she had "a desperate need for affection and a desperate need to give it". Perhaps the same was true of me at that age. In any case, I was generous in my affections and not a year went by without someone being the recipient of a heart-felt Valentine's card, which I sent despite the price I would inevitably pay in embarrassment not to mention of course the damage to my non-existent street-cred and reputation. However I was toughened by my early experiences of unrequited love and thanks to them I have become the hard-nosed career woman I am today!

Of course there are a thousand other memories of growing up by Balmaha: sitting selling daffodils to day-trippers at the bottom of the *Auchmar* drive; climbing the Conich in an antique ball-gown; dressing up as a birthday cake for the Queen's silver jubilee bonfire; trying to smoke the cigarettes the milkman had dropped; camping on Inchcailleach; playing cave-men by the rocks at the bottom of the Conich by *High Auchmar*; swimming and cutting your feet (all the time) at Manse Bay; cycling to Balmaha and beyond; seeing the white stag.

What is it like growing up by Balmaha? Ask a teenager and they'll tell you that without a car and a driver's license it's a living nightmare. But for kids before they're old enough to have an opinion, it has to be pretty good most of the time with plenty of scope for having nothing to do but homework (unless you live on a farm). And once you move beyond adolescence (which as we all know can last for anything from five to about fifty years) the appeal of living by Balmaha renews itself as you search for the peace, space, and beauty, which you can find there.

The Graham family on holiday in Cornwall, 1983. Hermione is flanked by Ronnie (left) and Jamie (right), Catherine and Seumas behind.
Photo Catherine Montrose

Betty Twaddle
Passfoot Cottage

Betty, Joe, and son Kevin moved to the University Field Station in 1966. Daughters Shona and Kirsty were born when they lived there and Kirsty was actually born at the Field Station itself. Betty went as a mature student to Stirling University 1979-83 and after a few years' temporary posts throughout the region, took up a permanent post teaching English at McLaren High School in Callander in 1987. Recently she decided to make the most of her home, Passfoot Cottage, and became, in the Parish's fine tradition, a B&B landlady.

Photo: Jenny Taggart

There is a fine tradition of 'Bed and Breakfast Ladies' in the Balmaha and Buchanan area. When my family and I arrived at the University Field Station in 1966 it was already a thriving industry. There was May Fraser and Nan Gow at the Forestry houses, Margaret Simpson at Cashel Farm, Jessie McLaren at *Critreoch* and of course, Annie and Jackie Frier in Balmaha.

Many of their clients came from far-flung places and some went off to far-flung places. Our daughter, Shona, went into a shop in Sidney, Australia. The proprietor recognised a Scottish accent, asked whereabouts in Scotland she came from. "Oh, just a wee village north of Glasgow." "Where?" he insisted. When she said "Balmaha" he told her how he used to stay with Nan Gow at some Forestry houses!

And these folk did come back year after year, a true test of hospitality given. The B&B ladies may have changed a number of times over the years but I hope we still maintain the high standards they set.

When the West Highland Way was officially opened in the early 80s, I think it was mostly walked by hardy back-packers who camped along the way – not without incurring some pretty serious blisters - as Bill Brennan, at Cashel Campsite could verify. Walkers seem much better prepared now and gradually the campers (though there are still many of them) have been overtaken or at least equalled by a clientele looking for a bit more comfort.

For the B&Bs, it is mostly walkers in the early months of the spring and summer, but as the season progresses it's not just the walkers. There is a range of guests from all over the world, all reminding me how lucky we are to live in such a beautiful spot and some making me feel guilty at my lack of knowledge. They know so much more about our history and culture. We had German guests staying at the same time as a young couple from Bishopbriggs. The young couple came back from The Oak Tree Inn full of awe for their German neighbours who had joined in with the band in the singing of Scottish songs – and knew all the words. We also had a young honeymoon couple from Moscow, Russia, and I think the only song on our *Hell for Leather* CD that they didn't know the words to was *Bonnie Balmaha*. How Jackie Frier would have loved to teach him. Rustan kept talking about how much he loved to read about all the bottles. I naturally thought he was referring to whisky, until he mentioned Bannockburn!

Not everyone is knowledgeable though. We had two couples from Birmingham who arrived with a boot load of supplies. They said they were not sure how far they were going from civilisation.

Certainly the creation of the National Park has raised awareness of our proximity to civilisation and of the special qualities of the area. But perhaps the biggest change in the life of the B&B industry has been the development of the Internet. At the click of the mouse guests can access all sorts of information and see exactly what is on offer.

But at the heart of the B&B industry are the guests and we look forward to the return of the fishermen, Albert and Ted, in September. They first came to Annie and Jackie's in the 1960s, we think. Even daughter Aggie can't remember a time without Albert and Ted's annual visit. Their photograph with their catch can be seen in The Oak Tree's collection. They're still as handsome but perhaps not quite so active. I think there might now be rather more reminiscing than fishing.

Agnes Frier in the 1960s.   *Photo: Willie Simpson*

Betty Twaddle

Bonnie Balmaha

Bonnie Balmaha

It lies beside Loch Lomond beneath my guiding star,
The place that seems so dear to me is Bonnie Balmaha,
The sunshine on Loch Lomond is brighter there by far,
And moonbeams play along the bay at Balmaha.

I look again towards the Ben, the steamers come and go,
The gentle breeze, the scent of trees and loch-shore fires aglow,
I know I'm only dreaming but be I near or far,
I'll aye give thanks for Lomond banks and Bonnie Balmaha.

I see the view so well I knew, the roadway winding by,
And seems to cheer the winter breer and lonely whiles am I,
I know I'm only dreaming yet be they near or far,
I'll aye give thanks to Lomond Banks and Bonnie Balmaha.

It lies beside Loch Lomond beneath my guiding star,
The place that seems so dear to me is Bonnie Balmaha,
The sunshine on Loch Lomond is brighter there by far,
And moonbeams play along the bay at Bonnie Balmaha.

Balmaha is described (by *Hell for Leather* on their CD '*Loch Lomond*') as "a small village on the east side of Loch Lomond where many good times have been had".
Words: Traditional.
Melody: courtesy of Peter Archibald of *Hell for Leather*.

Isobel Waddell
Buchanan Castle

Isobel Waddell has lived all her life in the Auld House next to Buchanan Castle Golf Course, where her father, Bill Bradford, was the first Head Greenkeeper. The Auld House *was originally part of the Buchanan family's country house and members of the Clan Buchanan come to view the house when researching their heritage.*

Isobel married husband John over forty years ago. Now retired, she worked for RS McColl as Financial Accounts Manager.

Photo: Jenny Taggart

I can just remember the pre-war Buchanan Castle Golf Club being a very busy place, particularly at the weekends, with lots of well dressed people arriving in expensive cars, expensive perfume, smells of delicious food and a general air of exciting things happening! I have a distant memory of being in the old tractor with my father when he was cutting the fairways but feeling 'seasick' with all the ups and downs. I also have vague memories of an exhibition game with Walter Hagen and another golfer who did lots of trick shots. My father was very strict as to where we were allowed to play and we just accepted this. Our front door was adjacent to the entrance to the Club and we were not allowed to clutter up this area with any toys or bikes. This was no great hardship as our interests were neither golf nor golfers – more likely to be games with children from The Smithy or the Home Farm or wandering in the woods and along the burns in the policies. I was the youngest and still pretty wee and the farthest I went was over to The Stables where a Miss Donald ran riding stables for the children of families who could afford this pastime. I loved the horses and made a nuisance of myself whenever I managed to escape my mother's attention. Sometimes I was allowed to sit on a pony when they were being led out to the field where they spent the night. At other times I had my own pony - a pair of mis-matched stirrups, some ropes and belts slung over a suitable branch and I rode for miles.

Isobel Waddell

When the *Castle* closed as a residence it seemed to be mothballed for some time and our neighbours Mr and Mrs. Fred Perryman moved up there to be caretakers. My next big memory is of watching the furniture from the *Castle* being brought down to The Stables for storage. This was exciting as anything that came from a castle had to be different from ordinary stuff and who knew what treasures might be seen. I was given a wee wooden doll with a hole through it and four nails on top for making woollen reins and a kaleidoscope both of which gave me hours of pleasure. For years afterwards that furniture held a fascination for us. We never accepted that there was nothing of interest for us in those storerooms.

Buchanan Castle in the 1930s.
Photo: Sandy Fraser

Then the building of the Military Hospital started and seemed to go on at quite a pace. The walks and ornamental gardens disappeared under foundations and brickwork. My brother and I certainly took and interest in all this but I think we must have scouted around in the evenings, as I don't remember being chased away. Then the personnel arrived, and while we were not encouraged to go up that way, I do not remember guards or anyone actually stopping us. We knew all the paths linking the various buildings, visited the fire pool where there were masses of newts and tadpoles and the little Church and also the mortuary on the bottom road which we regarded with some dread! The officers were, I think, allowed the use of the clubhouse and perhaps the golf course which had been reduced to eleven holes to allow for sheep grazing, and some bits ploughed up for crops.

My sister Betty took scarlet fever contracted from evacuees who stayed with us for a short time. She was quite ill and spent six weeks in Bannockburn Fever Hospital. The rest of us escaped infection but we suffered the fumigation of the house by, I think, sulphur candles being burned in every room and an excessive application of carbolic soap. These smells lingered on for ages in clothes, blankets and furnishings. Scarlet fever and also diphtheria were dangerous illnesses for children in the days before antibiotics and penicillin, so we were isolated from our friends and neighbours until the danger of infection was past.

After my father joined the army my mother was left on her own to keep things going. However, in spite of poor health, she was a most resourceful woman. She had worked in service as a young woman and when things became scarce she used her talents to good effect. She got hens, got us all involved in the vegetable plot, and continued to look after the bees which had been my father's hobby. She could cook, bake, sew and knit with the best of them. She made jam with any fruit she could lay hands on: wild brambles, rasps and rowans (not our favourite then although I love rowan jelly now) and local apples, rhubarb, plums and gooseberries. The hens were a mixed blessing as they laid away and also had to be chased into their henhouse every night instead of nesting in the bushes which they preferred. Their smelly henhouse also had to be cleaned out regularly, not a pleasant task and no pocket money reward given or expected! However, any young cockerels which were fattened up then killed for the table were a terrific treat, and no tears shed when they were dispatched by John Veitch the caddymaster and starter. The cockerels and the eggs were really free range as they had the freedom of the woods and both were delicious. The garden also produced lovely potatoes and vegetables although it was a fight to the death - gardeners versus rabbits, pigeons, pheasants etc.

The old Buchanan School.   *Photo: Jean Cummine*

I have many pleasant memories of Buchanan School after recovering from my initial shock of finding myself there at a very early age due to my mother's poor health. My first recollection is of changing my dress in the little cloakroom (stone floor and cold water) into a new one made by mum and matching my big sister's and made in a pretty forget-me-not blue cotton. Miss Jenny Johnston and Mrs Black were our much loved and greatly respected teachers at the little two roomed school.

As we got older, if we were good, we got to tidy up the stationery cupboard. This was a treasure house of new jotters, pencils and rubbers, and even now a new notebook or writing paper can take me back. The outside toilets were not for the faint hearted on a cold wet winter's day. I remember rushing round there one day with my lapbag on and managing to impale myself on four knitting needles on which I had been attempting to knit a sock. I also remember a trip to Edinburgh Zoo which stood out as a milestone as I don't think we ever went anywhere else. I also remember a writing competition, run by Ovaltine, where we had to copy out some lines of writing and I was thrilled to be told I had won a prize. This was a box of Ovaltine chocolate - dark and bitter. I must admit it was a bit of disappointment.

To and from school there was always something to watch, eat, pick or hear. We took shortcuts and diversions and were easily side tracked. We were occasionally late in the morning and always late home at night, always hungry and begging for a 'piece' to keep us going until dinner was on the table.

On the radio we listened to Children's Hour: *Down at the Mains*, *Tammy Troot* and *Larry the Lamb*. On a more sombre note, I also remember listening to *Into Battle*, which gave some idea of the progress of the war, and *The Man in Black* with Valentine Dyall which scared me stiff just before bed. In summer we might have games of 'kick the can' and 'hide and seek' with our pals from The Smithy or the Home Farm.

I remember the grown ups having Fire Drill in front of the stables with stirrup pumps, buckets of sand and long shovels to put out incendiary bombs. And I think the Estate fire engine, a very well preserved and handsome vehicle which was housed in a coach house in the stable yard, was also inspected at the drill. Thankfully none of these skills were ever put to the test.

My father, meantime, was making his way round the world, often uncomfortable, sometimes in danger, but thrilled to be seeing places and people he had only read about and never dreamed he would visit.

Isobel's father, Bill Bradford, on Buchanan Castle golf course.
Photo: Arthur Bayfield

At home, rationing was at its height, and how my mother kept us going with a small army pay and pretty basic rations I do not know. The Co-op grocer came once a week and what was delivered would be lost in one of today's supermarket baskets. I can still remember the list: butter, sugar, marge, lard, cheese, tea, soap, matches, and precious little else. Fortunately we transferred some books to Miss Bilsland in Drymen. She was very fair and gave us the chance of any extras that turned up: biscuit, tinned jam, dried fruit etc. The Co-op baker also called and we got enormous quantities of plain loaves all joined together and sometimes jam sandwich biscuits. Mr Gowans the baker in Drymen made lovely morning rolls which we sometimes had as a treat and I also have fond memories of his fresh cream cookies! However, most of the baked or cooked treats we had were made by mum using pretty basic equipment and spinning out our rations like magic. She had a little range, fuelled by coal, which heated the water and which was also provided an oven and top plates for cooking. From this she produced feasts, or so it seemed to us. Her other kitchen equipment consisted of a few pots, a frying pan and griddle, some ancient baking trays and cake tins, a really old beater for eggs and cream, measuring jug, spoons, knives and some old scales. I really can't recall much else. There was always a treat on the horizon – dumplings steamed in a bowl with silver threepenny bits for birthdays, pancakes, scones and cakes for family visitors, chips cooked in dripping and eaten out of paper pokey hats in front of the fire, treacle toffee, tablet or puff candy, brandy snaps curled over the rolling pin and filled with whipped cream, not to mention all the more everyday things that she made to fill us every day.

We didn't use the word 'recycle' in those days but we certainly practiced it. Clothes were taken up, let down, mended and darned. Woollens were ripped out and fashioned into another garment. I remember my sister when she started work sitting nearly every night darning the horrible lisle stockings which were all you could buy, then washing them through ready for the morning. Replacing broken china was also a problem. By the time things became more plentiful we were down to a pretty sorry collection of odds and ends, mostly quite thick and off-white. Even now I find it hard to discard things which might still have a bit of life in them.

When things were scarce we were sometimes excited to receive a parcel from relations in Canada. We didn't get many parcels so unwrapping it was saved until everyone was there. It might contain cake mix, Jell-o, dried fruit, sweets and some clothes which unfortunately never fitted me, so the organdie party dress and silver shoes were never worn – too tight. At some part of the war we were required to billet a land girl. I have quite a strong recollection of this girl who seemed very sophisticated and smart to me. I expect that she was like a fish out of water with us as she had a pretty spartan billet. She shared our perishing bathroom and left behind her nice perfumes of scent and soap but what she did for meals I don't remember.

Later we had a couple named Mr & Mrs Bonfils. The husband did not sound French, but his wife had a very pronounced accent although her English was considerably better than our French. They were very pleasant and got to share our still perishing bathroom. Our little dog liked popping up to visit them to pick up some little treats of meat or cheese when available, especially as sometimes all she got for dinner at that time was saps (bread and milk).

At some time many of the beautiful trees on the Estate were felled. The big trees had made it easy to walk through the woods but now the birches, rhodies, willow herb and other weeds quickly took over. The walks and paths quickly became overgrown although we did our bit to keep them open trailing up and down the burn, guddling for fish, visiting the grotto which was still beautifully lined with hazel sticks patterns in the walls and ceiling, the wee dam under which we sometimes found the biggest fish and visiting the grave of a favourite horse of one of the Dukes. This was marked by a wooden gravestone giving details of the horse, but now, sadly, the board has rotted away. The quarry was another magnet for us. It held the Estate sawmill, wood stores, cart sheds and various other outhouses which were full of all sorts of things stored there until required. I don't think there was much that we could have damaged but it was out of bounds. There was a little pond where a duck always nested and the best primroses were to be found in the cliff above the pond, and so we risked life and limb trying to get to them. At some later date waste from the *Castle* was dumped there and set on fire. This was dangerous because it looked OK on the surface but was burning away underneath, something my brother learned to his cost. He burned his foot badly. It was extremely painful and took ages to heal.

Funeral of the sixth Duke of Montrose, 1954. *Photo: Sandy Fraser*

Buchanan Smithy was another fascinating place. We used to watch the big carthorses being shod by Mr Tom Anderson and his brother Davie. The big horses were usually quiet and patient but we had heard tales of wild and dangerous beasts so we were kept at a safe distance. It was an exciting place with the fire, the bellows, the noise of hammering and the smell of burnt hooves and the horrible murky bath where the hot shoes were cooled in the filthy looking water.

We had some very cold winters with long spells of deep frost with huge icicles, burns frozen over, frozen pipes and bursts. It was exciting during the day but not so comfortable later when all our efforts went into keeping the water running and keeping ourselves warm. During these cold spells our bedrooms were freezing although occasionally we would be allowed to have a wee coal fire in the small black fireplaces which were a relic of the days when our house was perhaps part of the nursery wing of the *Auld House*. There were no electric blankets but we might have a stone piggy or a heated flat iron wrapped in an old woollen jumper. All this with only linoleum on the floor and just a bedside rug - still we never seemed to be any the worse for these spartan conditions.

There are sights and sound which I enjoyed in my childhood which have almost disappeared – the sound of larks, oystercatchers and corncrake and strangely enough sparrows and starlings which used to be so numerous. I only occasionally hear a curlew these days although they used to nest regularly on the golf course. We now have magpies, buzzards and foxes in increasing numbers although I don't remember any of these when I was a youngster. Hares, which used to be such a common and amusing sight on the golf course, are seldom seen and the burns, which used to teem with wee trout, 'baggies' and 'beardies' are strangely empty now. I never hear a cockerel and few people can be bothered to keep hens.

Writing down these bits and pieces from my childhood has brought home to me how much I remember through the senses - conversations, thoughts and feelings seem to have faded or been overtaken by later events. But it only takes a smell, a sound or a taste to spark off some memory from the past. Also, as a child, I never thought of things changing. Time went slowly and the people and places that I knew would always be the same. Buchanan (and Drymen) would always be the School, the Church, the Post Office, Dr. Maud, Willie Kirk's, Crowe's Tearoom, Gowans the baker, Mason's garage and the bank. Some of them are still there but in a different guise.

We had tremendous freedom to roam about the countryside and no one seemed to think that we were threatened in any way. Everyone we met was known to our parents. Few people had cars and anyway petrol was in short supply for a number of years so our horizons were limited to within a few miles of home. Whether what we had was better than nowadays is hard to say. There were hardships and shortages and many worries and cares for our parents and even children were afraid of air raid alerts and the sound of what might be enemy planes. In spite of this I feel that I had a very happy childhood in a very beautiful and tranquil place with good friends and neighbours.

Ruthie Wiberg
Sallochy

Ruthie Russell Ferguson lived at Sallochy House *until she was eighteen years of age. Her father was the local councillor serving on Stirling County Council from 1954 -1969 with a break of only three years. In 1932 her mum was the* Women's Own *first ever cover girl. Ruthie is married to Jim Wiberg and lives in Glasgow. She works a Social Research Interviewer and still keeps her links with the Buchanan community through the Church.*

Photo: Ruthie Wiberg

My early years were spent with my family at *Sallochy House* about three miles before Rowardennan. I was an infant just after the war and I am told that German POWs came to help with the tattie howking. One in particular always insisted on clicking his heels and saluting me as I lay in my pram. My very young memories include playing in the foundations of what would become the Forestry cottages, and I am told that several small dolls probably had a concrete burial after I forgot to take them home. Collecting nuts and bolts from the recently demolished ammunition huts was also a regular pastime.

Some of my most abiding memories are of extremes in weather; summers were endlessly sunny and the winters were fierce. Being snowed in was a non-event. Since nobody had freezers in those days and as our fridge was less than efficient, fresh meat was stored in airtight and animal proof tins and left by the back door in the snow. Flour, lentils, potatoes, root veggies and other staples were bought on the grand scale, probably three stones of spuds and much the same of carrots and turnips at a time, although we did grow some vegetables ourselves. In the summer, we played in the garden, hatless after babyhood and without sun cream, but never seemed to suffer.

A lot of shopping was done from travelling vans. Bobby came from Buchlyvie to Rowardennan once or twice a week with his butcher's van, and if we were VERY good, we were allowed to inspect the sheep's head on the front seat. Posties Alex Stewart and Archie Dow provided a free delivery service for local mail to Rowardennan and collected outgoing mail on the way down. They would also give lifts to local people on a first come first served basis.

With no immediate neighbours, my sister Hélène and I made our own entertainment, dressing up and presenting plays to our long-suffering parents was a favourite. Then there was the bridge over the stream on the way down to the Loch. Having read the story of the *Billy Goats Gruff*, we became acutely aware of the Trolls that might just live under that bridge and it had to be crossed at speed. We messed about in the stream, built dams, caught minnows and tiddlers, guddled for the occasional trout. Once I jumped into a pool that was deeper than my wellies were high. Screaming to dad that I was about to drown, he picked me out and upended me. In the spring we collected tadpoles from a pool near what is now the Forestry Campsite at Cashel, but quickly lost interest as they took far too long to mature. Later in the year, we collected rosehips to take to school, to be made into rose hip syrup for children.

Hunting for tadpoles in a Lochside burn.   *Photo: Jenny Taggart*

To get to school, we travelled by school bus, driven by Dochie McLaren and then Tommy Kerr, the gears grinding as it chuntered up and down the hills. We slid down the Pass on our satchels when the road was icy. Starting school was a great adventure, although I recall being a bit scared of the big boys (probably age nine or ten), especially on the ice slide in the playground, which ended in the coal heap. At break times we slithered down the mudslide to reach the burn where we played, completely unsupervised.

Certainly nobody drowned and I don't remember many people getting seriously soaked. If we did get wet, there was a warm school to dry out; the smell of socks steaming on the stove in Miss Ewan's classroom while we had singing lessons, *Rhythm and Melody* and *Singing Together*, courtesy of the BBC Schools Programme. The walk-in cupboard off the senior classroom was always viewed with trepidation; not only was it for storage, it was also where Crabbit Chrissie gave people the belt. The shadow of the belt visible through the glass door was a good deterrent! Mrs Forbes doled out large portions of what was probably very unsuitable food for growing children, but we ate it and it didn't seen to do us any harm. After lunch, when we were older, we were allowed to cross the road and play in the shelter. I also remember having piano lessons from the Minister's wife, Grace Fulton, in what seemed a very large, very cold, manse.

Highlights of the year included the Annual Flower Show where mum bought a lot of local produce, and Drymen Show where I was extremely envious of my cousin who had a pony and took part in the gymkhana events. My only experience of owning a pony was when I cycled to Cashel Farm and traded my bike for Dixie. Proudly, I rode him home bareback, but alas, it was not to be. Within hours, the pony had thrown me, stood on my father's foot and bitten my sister's hand. Cashel was phoned and told I would be returning the pony and could I please have my bike back!

Buchanan Flower Show; Ian Hay (left) and Duncan MacFadyen.   *Photo: Willie Simpson*

In the early 1960s life changed completely for those beyond Balmaha. We got mains electricity. Until that time our electricity came from a generator that dad said ran on whisky. Gone were the days of having to make sure your torch had power to last the night in case you needed to go to the loo. Gone were the days of cleaning your teeth in the burn when the supply pipes iced up. Gone were the days when we had to turn off lights all the time as the more lights were on the dimmer they became. Mum had to do the ironing during the day; otherwise we would have been in darkness. We now had television, albeit with pretty poor reception from Northern Ireland, central heating, a washing machine, a toaster which toasted both sides of a slice at the same time, an electric kettle and best of all from a teenager's point of view, a dishwasher. I was at home when the SSEB came up to install the cables that summer. One glorious sunny day my father nobbled the foreman and invited him up to *Sallochy* for a beer or two. Looking out over Loch Lomond, dad casually commented what a shame it would be to spoil such a view with electricity cables crossing it. The point was taken, and that is why the mains cables run underground from the bottom of the hill to just beyond *Sallochy House*.

Age nine and being sent to boarding school near Balfron was a very difficult experience from starting at Buchanan but, if nothing else, it did teach me to appreciate the idyllic place where I lived, being driven home for a day or weekend out and doing a mental "Wow" as we turned the corner at the Forestry camping ground. The field at Cashel was in the process of being converted into the campsite, but before it was occupied by tents and caravans, this was where I had my first driving lesson in a Standard Vanguard. Reversing in and out of the individual pitches was good practice for real roads, but I never discovered why my father insisted I had to change to second gear to go up Critreoch hill whatever speed I was doing.

With no public transport, cycling was our main method of getting around. In those days the *Maid of the Loch* called at both Balmaha and Rowardennan, so for a big expedition a decision had to made which route was best as both directions involved hills. The favoured route was from Balmaha to Rowardennan as the Rowardennan-Balmaha route had both the Pass and the steep Critreoch hill to climb on the way home.

Maid of the Loch.   *Photo: Internet*

Then there was the Dramatic Club. As a child I enjoyed watching plays, but now was my chance to take part. We produced one play a year, mostly three act farces by William Douglas-Home or W Somerset Maugham, and we once entered the Scottish Community Drama Association Festival with Anton Chekov's *The Jubilee*.

My father was Commodore of the Clyde Canoe Club, now Loch Lomond Sailing Club, so we were taught the rudiments of sailing at an early age. This was not really enjoyed by either my sister or me, as dad was of the school of "I have told you before to do this/not do that", and didn't mind raising his voice while he told us, but our lessons were abruptly curtailed after dad's demonstration of where not to stand on a boat, and it capsized. Two children were absolutely delighted, but had huge difficulty trying to keep our faces straight while making appropriate noises of consolation.

Things were slowly changing, not always for the best. The road was a lot busier with Glaswegians out for a run in the country. White lines appeared, and Dad complained one day that he had to wait to cross the road. In the 1970s the only shop and petrol pumps at Balmaha vanished, and the Tearoom burned down. As society became more affluent, a lot of Glasgow commuters arrived in the district, and the area began to lose some of its local charm. Some contributed to the community, but for the majority it was purely a dormitory and they preferred to do their shopping and socialise in Glasgow rather than locally.

John Maxwell of Cashel.   *Photo: Willie Simpson*